What Leaders Are Saying

"There is increasing evidence that Protestant Christians are waking up to the efficacy of prayer for healing. David Smith's book is an important contribution to the Christian healing ministry."

Lyle W. Dorsett, Billy Graham professor of
evangelism, Beeson Divinity School

"Balanced, practical advice from a mature pastor who avoids both the overpromise and the underuse that often mar the healing gifts. Thoughtful biblical guidance on what to do before, during and after healing—or its delay—in the context of a loving local church."

Russell P. Spittler, provost, Vanguard University;
provost emeritus, senior professor of New Testament,
Fuller Theological Seminary

"*How Can I Ask God for Physical Healing?* is the most unique book on divine healing on the market today! While most books on healing are written for theologians and practitioners, this thoroughly biblical and highly practical book walks the person who longs for healing into a deeper faith and a stronger commitment to Christ our Healer. I highly recommend *How Can I Ask God for Physical Healing?* Every church should have multiple copies. Every pastor and elder needs to read it, but churches also need copies at the ready to give to those who are ill and long to be made whole. Use its principles and you will see more healings in your church!"

Jonathan Graf, president, Church Prayer Leaders Network;
founding editor, *Pray!* magazine

How Can I
Ask God *for*
PHYSICAL HEALING?

a biblical guide

DAVID J. SMITH

Chosen

Grand Rapids, Michigan

© 2005 by David J. Smith

Published by Chosen Books
a division of Baker Publishing Group
P.O. Box 6287, Grand Rapids, MI 49516-6287
www.chosenbooks.com

Printed in the United States of America

Library of Congress Cataloging-in-Publication Data
Smith, David J., 1953–
    How can I ask God for physical healing? : a biblical guide / David
J. Smith.
        p.   cm.
    Includes bibliographical references and index.
    ISBN 0-8007-9392-7 (pbk.)
    1. Spiritual healing. 2. Healing—Religious aspects—Christianity.
I. Title.
BT732.5.S62 2005
234′.131—dc22   2005003280

To my wife, Donna,

whom God has given to me

through whom God often speaks

to whom I have learned to listen

Contents

Introduction: *The Journey toward Physical Healing* 9

Section One: *Before Prayer for Healing*

1. Need: *What Is Your Need?* 19
2. Want: *What Do You Want Jesus to Do for You?* 23
3. Lessons: *What Is God Teaching You through This Affliction?* 30
4. Scripture: *What Do You Believe the Bible Says about Healing?* 38
5. Love: *Does God Really Love You?* 52
6. Faith: *Will God Heal You and Heal You at This Time?* 58
7. Cause: *What Is the Underlying Cause of Your Sickness?* 65
8. Barriers: *Are You Removing Barriers to Healing?* 76
9. Deliberation: *Have You Thoroughly Prepared Your Inner Life?* 84
10. Commitment: *Are You Ready to Give Yourself Totally to God?* 91

Section Two: *During Prayer for Healing*

11. Readiness: *Which Scriptures Are You Claiming for Your Healing?*   101
12. Others: *Have You Called Others to Pray?*   110
13. Ask: *Are You Ready to Ask God to Heal You Now?*   118
14. Authority: *Do You Need to Exercise Authoritative Faith?*   123
15. Sensations: *Are There Further Triggers of Faith That God Gives?*   131
16. Encounter: *Is Your Authentic Faith Leading to an Encounter with the Risen Christ?*   137

Section Three: *After Prayer for Healing*

17. Do: *Are You Believing and Acting As Though God Has Healed You?*   149
18. Trials: *Are You Prepared for Trials of Faith?*   159
19. Abide: *Are You Continuing to Draw Life from the Risen Christ?*   165
20. Providence: *Are You Trusting Christ Even if He Has Not Healed You?*   171
21. Living: *After Your Healing, Are You Living a Changed Life?*   185
22. Purpose: *Are You Using Your New Strength and Health for God?*   194

Appendix 1: The Healing Ministry of Jesus Christ in the Gospels   201
Appendix 2: The Healing Ministry in the Church Today   204
Notes   212
Index   218

Introduction

The Journey toward Physical Healing

You want to be healed. Or you know someone who does. You have heard that God heals in answer to faith expressed in prayer. But how do you get there?

Many Americans (86 percent) believe that prayer heals people. Many doctors (75 percent) believe that prayer can bring patients to greater health. Many family physicians (in one study, 99 percent of 269 polled) report a belief that religious practices can be a valuable element of the healing process. More and more, therapists and doctors are recognizing that spiritual interventions succeed where other methods fail. The number of medical schools offering courses in topics about healing and spirituality has gone from three to sixty in five years.

But how does healing prayer work?

Mention the word *healing* and some Christians become overly enthusiastic. Others grow cautious. But when you are sick, you wish for only one thing: You want to get better. You pray desperately, and press others to pray, for God to work through the doctors. You pray earnestly for God to make the medications and treatments effective. You pray fervently for God to touch your body supernaturally.

Yet you have numerous questions about healing: How can I ask God for healing? Is there a path to divine healing? Does Jesus still heal today? Will Jesus heal me and heal me now?

Your mind wrestles with the issues: What if people pray and nothing happens? Or what if people pray and something *does* happen . . . *what then*?

A Pastoral Guide

I want to talk with you about your physical need. Perhaps you have come to my office where we can speak openly about your honest questions. Perhaps we are having a phone conversation about an urgent request. Perhaps I am pulling a chair alongside your hospital bed. I want to talk with you as a pastor, friend, counselor, confidant, guide.

Having served as a pastor for more than twenty years, I have noticed that hardly a week goes by without somebody mentioning a new prayer request for someone's physical need. I have seen people healed in answer to prayer. People have told me their stories of how Christ touched them.

Yet I have also seen that many Christians do not know how to respond to the written Word of God or how to appropriate the inner movements of God's Spirit prompting them to see Christ as their Healer. They do not know how to seek the Lord prayerfully for their healing.

Christian classics on healing continue to sell by such authors as Francis MacNutt, F. F. Bosworth and Agnes Sanford. Works on healing from the Holiness stream include A. B. Simpson, A. J. Gordon and Andrew Murray. Some recent Christian publishing trends have focused on inner healing or healing from a medical or nutritional viewpoint.

While many authors say many important things about healing, my goal here is to provide you with specific pastoral how-tos for prayerfully approaching the Lord as the Healer of your body. I want to guide you as you wrestle with your questions about how faith works. I want to help you lift your wavering heart to God. I want to show you how to place your trembling hands into the strong hands of the Great Physician. Jesus Christ can and does heal today.

How Can I Ask God for Physical Healing? is a step-by-step guide for exercising your faith in God for physical healing. I want to lead you into a biblically balanced, faith-filled approach of prayer for healing in three ways:

- Providing simple yet thorough steps leading into prayer for healing
- Suggesting how to activate faith when others pray for you
- Counseling on what to do after prayer for healing

You will experience some touch from God. He will honor your seeking heart in some way—a physical healing, an emotional healing, an increase of faith, a greater love for God, a deeper sense of peace. *This is because prayer for healing is primarily a spiritual encounter with the risen Christ!*

A Model for Healing

As you may know, Christians approach healing in various ways. Some emphasize dynamic healing evangelists. Others exercise charismatic gifts of healing. Still others use guided liturgical practices. These models all have their places in the ministry of healing.

11

I am working from a model that stresses the importance of the prayers of fellow believers in the healing process. This model is derived from a familiar New Testament passage:

> Is any one of you sick? He should call the elders of the church to pray over him and anoint him with oil in the name of the Lord. And the prayer offered in faith will make the sick person well; the Lord will raise him up. If he has sinned, he will be forgiven. Therefore confess your sins to each other and pray for each other so that you may be healed. The prayer of a righteous man is powerful and effective.
>
> James 5:14–16

With this Scripture as our model, we will approach healing ministry with three presuppositions:

1. *Local Church*—The primary vehicle for the regular practice of the healing ministry is the ministry of the local church. This is not to say, of course, that the only place you can pray for healing is in a church building. Prayer ministry can take place in a hospital, a home, anywhere. Prayer for healing also does not have to be limited to the particular people with whom you attend church on Sunday; perhaps you are part of a close-knit Bible study or neighborhood home group that believes in the power of healing prayer. The important thing is that this ministry be centered where people know each other, are accountable to each other as brothers and sisters in Christ and genuinely care for one another before and after prayer for healing. I have found, indeed, that this generally is most likely to occur in the local church.

2. *Trusted Believers*—The central role of trusted believers is crucial in the healing ministry. God often uses those who are seasoned in the church and in faith. These people may be spiritual leaders like pastors or elders or deacons. They may be small group leaders, counselors or ministry leaders. They may also be parents praying for their children or friends praying for their friends. You trust these people spiritually because they have a connection with God and they care for you. They will pray with authority and you know it. The Lord uses the prayers of these ordinary Christians in extraordinary ways.

3. *Christ Encounter*—The principal focus of those seeking healing should be Christ as the Healer. It should not be those doing the praying and it should not be the presence or absence of feelings or manifestations. The goal for those seeking healing is to encounter the risen Lord Jesus Christ. God then gets the focus and the credit.

A Pattern for Prayer

As you seek the Lord for healing, I will lead you prayerfully, step by step, through three broad phases. I suggest you think of healing with a before, during and after approach.

- *Before*—What steps can you take to prepare your heart for healing? How can you cultivate faith prior to the ministry of prayer by other believers? How can you get ready to receive a genuine touch from God?
- *During*—What do you do when trusted believers pray for you? Do you just sit there like a bug and

13

expect God to zap you? How can you activate your faith while others pray?

- *After*—What do you do after prayer for your healing? How do you continue to nurture your faith for healing? What should you do when God *does* heal you, and what specific steps of faith can you take if God *does not* heal you?

In every chapter I will direct you toward key Scriptures, provide thorough explanations, offer helpful illustrations and stories, and conclude with reflection questions and a prayer.

While I discuss these uncomplicated "steps," I freely admit the mystery of healing—that God does not heal everyone completely all the time in this present age. When we follow biblically inspired steps, Jesus always honors us with some measure of healing to body, mind or spirit. Yet following these steps does not guarantee physical healing. Jesus is the Healer, not some formula.

Still, I believe the Lord wants to heal many more people than are healed. Jesus Himself posed the question: "When the Son of Man comes, will he find faith on the earth?" (Luke 18:8). I trust you want to know how to have that kind of faith. What Jesus did in New Testament times, He still does today, for "Jesus Christ is the same yesterday and today and forever" (Hebrews 13:8). Even as a light bulb begins to blaze the instant it connects with the power source, so we experience God's presence and power the moment we reach out to touch Jesus as our Healer.

My hope and prayer are that you will encounter the risen Lord Jesus Christ for your body. That His wonderful love will touch you. That His mighty power will heal you, your family, your friends. And while this book is about healing, I dare not overlook the gift greater than healing—Jesus as our Savior. Jesus wants to make people "whole." This is what "being saved" is all about.

Physical healing is only a part of the greater miracle of a changed life. Let me tell you a personal story.

Jesus Touched Me!

While just starting a new pastoral ministry in 2000, I sensed God prompting me to ask the elders of my church to pray for me. I had had a knot of muscles between my shoulders for close to two years and could not lift my left arm without difficulty and pain. When the elders prayed in faith for me, I reached out to Jesus in faith to take healing from Him. As they prayed, the knot in my back relaxed. The suddenness of this sensation surprised me. The rest of that Sunday afternoon I felt my back continuing to relax. A month later, I testified that I was on the "very much improvement" scale. In time the knot and the discomfort in my back were completely gone! I knew Jesus touched me!

Let me walk with you on this spiritual journey for physical healing. Lift your eyes to heaven. As you move forward prayerfully, be listening to God's Spirit. Not every step may be important for you. But work your way through these progressive steps. The ones that stand out are the ones in which you need to spend time with the Lord. Then when you are ready to move forward, go for it.

Begin to open your heart now for the wonder God intends to do.

Reflections

1. What are some questions you have about healing?
2. Whom do you know who needs a divine touch from the risen Jesus?
3. How is the Lord stirring your heart to believe that He will do something great, something mighty?

Prayer

Father God, as I begin this spiritual journey toward physical healing, cause me to see You in a fresh way. Help me believe You will do something great, something mighty. Here I am. Take my hand. Walk with me. Guide me. Grant me the graces I need. I hunger for this adventure to draw me closer to You whatever the result.

Section One

Before Prayer for Healing

What happens when you as a believer in Jesus become physically sick? What goes through your mind? What are you feeling inside? What internal movements of God take place? How are you processing your condition as you consider the possibility of healing? Your movement toward healing initiates the first phase: personal preparation.

1
Need

What Is Your Need?

The first step toward healing is acknowledging that you have a physical problem and need a divine touch from the Savior. What seems obvious may not be. Initiating a series of heart-searching questions is normal and desirable when you come to God for physical healing. You may begin asking yourself and the Lord what the problem is. You recognize something in your body is not functioning right. You don't feel good. You feel pain. Some symptom prompts legitimate concern. You begin to look to God.

You might discover your physical need is symptomatic of a deeper spiritual need. You might find yourself entering a deeper level of your faith journey. You might be learning how God has uniquely fashioned you, integrating your mind, body and spirit. I would estimate that perhaps sixty percent or more of seekers struggle with an issue of the soul. But right now your body is trying to tell you something. You don't feel healthy! What is your *need*?

What part of your body hurts? Is it internal or external? Does your concern relate to your digestive, nervous or respiratory system? Did you break a bone? Do you have muscle pain? Are you fighting a virus or an infection? Is it your heart, your brain or your limbs that concern you? Have you sought medical advice? What did the doctor say? Something plainly in the structure or function of your human body is at risk. Someone possibly has helped you identify a genuine physical problem. In some way you have begun to distinguish between symptom and ailment. Again, what specifically is your *need*?

The Whole You

In one way or another, you have acknowledged that you are indeed sick in some way and in need of some kind of cure. God's ideal standard for people is health and wholeness in every respect. Sickness means that you are less than whole.

In our Western culture, we often splinter body, soul and spirit into separate entities. While these categories are helpful in understanding certain human aspects, your soul is not walking around separate from your body! Your inner life is not detached from its outer container. You are a whole person. You do not have a body; you are a body. You do not have a soul or a spirit; you are a soul and you are a spirit. This is you, the whole you. You are an integrated person whom God has designed. God does not delight in your soul and disregard your body. Clement of Alexandria (ca.150–215), an early Christian theologian and philosopher, stated, "The all-sufficient Physician of humanity, the Saviour, heals both body and soul."[1] Yes, the Lord loves the whole you.

A Quest for a Cure

A sick body is, therefore, not normal. A sick body is not the perfect expression of God's presence in your life. Even human nature tells us to avoid physical pain, suffering, weakness and the shortening of life. Even human nature prompts us to do whatever we can to deliver ourselves from these conditions. Ignoring a problem will not make it disappear. Indeed, the Lord Jesus taught us to pray, "Deliver us from evil" (Matthew 6:13, KJV). *My point is this: If you deny that you have a physical need, then you will not engage in a quest for a cure.*

Perhaps men are guiltier of saying, "I'm okay—I'm all right," when pain (and maybe a concerned wife) is screaming at them to pay attention to a physical need. Rick Wallace, our Student Ministries Pastor, provides a good example from his father. For years the children pressed their father to see a doctor about his persistent cough. But he resisted, fooling himself, thinking he was okay. Finally, he went to a doctor, discovered a spot on his lungs, fortunately not cancer, and received treatment.

Yes, it is a significant step to say honestly, "I have a problem that I can't solve. I have a physical need that I can't remedy. I need help. This is what I need." Absolute honesty is required for everyone seeking divine healing.

Admitting Your Need

One day when Jesus was going into a village, ten men who had leprosy met Him. Luke tells us: "They stood at a distance and called out in a loud voice, 'Jesus, Master, have pity on us!' When he saw them, he said, 'Go, show yourselves to the priests.' And as they went, they were cleansed" (Luke 17:12–14).

These men knew they had a serious problem: Their ugly skin disease was obvious to all. They had bonded together because of their similar ailment and their common experience of alienation from others. In calling out to Jesus they were acknowledging their desperate physical state. From a distance they cried out, "Jesus, Master, have pity on us!"

Their humble request for mercy was enough to trigger a response from the Master. It is interesting that Jesus neither approached them nor touched them. Neither did He say, "Be healed," nor did He affirm, "You are cured!" He did, however, direct them to follow the normal procedure for a leper who was cured: "Go, show yourselves to the priests." They had expressed their need, and now they responded in obedience. When they acted as though they had been cured, God cleansed them.

As we begin this journey toward healing, what am I calling you toward from the very beginning? Essentially, I want you to identify your condition. State your physical need as precisely and accurately as you can. Admit that you need a cure. Tell Jesus you love Him and believe in Him. Call upon the Lord for mercy.

Reflections

1. Are you willing to admit that you have a physical need or are you still struggling with denial?
2. What exactly is your physical need? Can you describe it in concrete terms?
3. Have you sought medical advice? Do you freely admit that you need a cure, even a divine cure, if you are going to get better?

Prayer

God, what is going on here? What I am feeling physically is not right. Something is wrong with my body, and I do not like it. I admit that I have this physical problem and need a cure. Here is my concern. . . . This is what my specific need is. . . . Lord Jesus Christ, Son of God, have mercy on me.

22

2
Want

What Do You Want Jesus to Do for You?

If God were to give you *your miracle*, what would it look like? Smell like? Taste like? Feel like? Sound like? Have you spent enough time in the presence of God to crystallize what you want? Can you see it?

This is important because your desire will determine how you pray. While I was a student at seminary, for instance, my wife and I prayed for a car. Our desire shaped our specific prayer: "God, we need a car—one recommended by *Consumer Reports*, four-door, automatic transmission, air-conditioning, cruise control, right price." More on that request in a moment.

Crystallizing Your Desire

Discerning what a person wants was at the heart of Jesus' question to the blind beggar sitting by the roadside (see Luke 18:35–43). As Jesus approached Jericho, the noisy excitement of a gathering crowd drew the attention of this blind man. He had to look through others' eyes to learn what was happening. Jesus was passing by, they told him. Looking from sightless spheres, his mind was in a whirl. He had only *heard* that this Jesus had healed many sick and crippled people. He had only *heard* that the masses regarded this Jesus as the Messiah. In spite of those who tried to quiet him, seizing the moment, he took his best shot to receive mercy. "Jesus, Son of David!" he shouted out.

Jesus stopped. A cry for mercy is good, but a cry for mercy is not necessarily enough. Everybody wants mercy sometime. After the blind beggar was brought to Him, Jesus asked pointedly, "What do you want me to do for you?" *Once asked, his desire crystallized.* He was not hoping to be pitied. No longer did he seek a general blessing for his welfare. His faith request went straight to the point. "Lord, I want to *see.*" It was as clear and simple and direct as Jesus' question.

Jesus then said to him, "Receive your sight; your faith has healed you." Dramatically, Luke tells us that "immediately he received his sight." His faith did not produce the cure, but it was the path from which he received a cure from God. Healed of his blindness, he praised God while others joined the celebration. The blind man *wanted* to see, and he *did not want* to be blind anymore! He got from God the specific answer he wanted.

Cultivating What You Want

You would think that the dizzying power of desire would draw people like a magnet to Christ for healing. But some people have little desire to be healed. They may even enjoy their sickness. They may like the attention they receive because of their maladies. They may relish wallowing in self-pity. These are big barriers. Harold Nicolson (1886–1968), English writer and politician, admitted, "One of the minor pleasures in life is to be slightly ill."[1]

Others have scarcely nurtured their desires or hopes. They only "wish" to be healed. So they are only as healed as they *wish* to be. *Healing—it would be nice, so they think. I wouldn't mind feeling a little better.* It has not occurred to them, apparently, to light and fan into a steady flame what they really *want* from God. The Lord does not answer "wishes" but requests. He says, "Ask!"

Still others misdirect their desires for healing. They seek healing for a minor physical need, when they could seek the Lord for a greater healing. Someone may pray, "Lord, please take away this headache," when that person really needs healing from a tumor or a broken leg! The deeper needs of the body are overlooked. Is your God too small?

Faith has a focus. I mentioned above our need for a car while I was a struggling seminary student. "God, we need a car—one recommended by *Consumer Reports*, four-door, automatic transmission, air-conditioning, cruise control, right price." And God answered our specific prayer in every detail! A shiny red Dodge Colt! Certainly not a luxury car, but a car that met our needs and kept going until we were in a church ministry.

Let me ask you: Specifically, what do you *want* Jesus to do for you? This is a huge faith factor. Weak desires can keep you from considering or seeking or expecting God to heal you. Sift through your chaos of pain. Sift through your anxiety of emotions. Find your heart's desire. *Let your driving motivation be, "Lord, I want to be healed!"*

Resisting What You Don't Want

Similarly, you have to resist the evil of your sickness. On the one hand, you are nurturing a desire to be healed. On the other hand, you are fighting back the illness.

Doctors are realizing that faith has a role in the healing process. They affirm, for example, that those who fight cancer with faith live longer.

Some well-meaning Christians have unwisely encouraged other believers to embrace their sickness as an angel from God, rather than to resist it as an enemy. Yet even when Job accepted his plight from the hand of God, he didn't like it. Sickness is a curse, an infirmity, a weakness, an affliction, a bondage, an enemy. It has the smell of death. To resist it is both natural and spiritual.

It is biblical to take your stand against sorrow, sickness and calamity. It is spiritual to hold your position steadily. Are you developing an attitude of resistance against your condition? Are you choosing not to succumb to it? Are you refusing to accept it as an inevitable necessity? *Take your stand against your illness. Hold your ground firmly. Refuse to yield or retreat.*

This is not merely a mental game. When I first entered pastoral ministry, I served with a senior pastor, the Rev. Duane Morscheck. God often used him in the ministry of healing. He pointed out that the longer it takes to begin resisting our sickness, the longer we have allowed a lack of faith to gain hold. The time lag between the acknowledgment of our need and the expression of our desire is an omission of faith. True faith ascends quickly when the sickness is refused.

For example, the moment you feel a sore throat coming on, you should resist it, pray against it and ask God to deliver you from it. Your faith says that you want something very much, and your faith says equally that you do not want whatever is causing this distress. You *want* Jesus to touch you and make you well, and you *do not want* this sickness to afflict you anymore.

Refining Your Desires

You must want God to heal you. You must be motivated to go after it specifically. Desire alone, of course, is not the only faith factor. You must also aggressively ask, seek and knock. Yet *wanting* is an important part of receiving the Lord's touch in your body. At times your desire will be intense, desperate and persistent.

We must note, however, that the desire for receiving physical healing and the desire for ridding ourselves of physical suffering, however intense, may not result in healing. Strong desires do not heal us; Christ Jesus heals us. When our desires are unfulfilled, and when God has apparently said no, we can find consolation in Christ's death on the cross. God did not exempt our Lord from suffering, pain and death. He "endured the cross, scorning its shame" (Hebrews 12:2). He did not enjoy His suffering. Instead He looked "for the joy set before him." Rather than let the condition become a stumbling block, we "fix our eyes on Jesus, the author and perfecter of our faith." Because Christ endured the cross, we can accept our condition. Only do not accept this position too soon.

Here is my advice: *Seek to be healed until God either heals you or gives you an answer as to why you are not healed.* God may be refining your desires. *Why* do you want to be healed? Why do you want *God* to heal you? Perhaps you are saying: "I'm sick and tired of being sick and tired! I can't bear this pain any longer! Enough is enough!"

Or if you are a parent, grandparent or caregiver for someone in need, your family most likely depends on your functioning as fully as possible. Your church or community may count on you to continue in some ministry. I have often heard people say, "Pastor, the reason I am still alive is because God still has a purpose for my life."

Or maybe you can honestly say that you want to be healed so God may be glorified. As a believer in Jesus, your underlying motivation for healing is ultimately for the pleasure of God and the glory of Christ. To please God rather than waste a life on selfish pleasures and pride is what you want. As the Lord purifies your desires and *you want* what God wants, you may discover to your delight that *God wants* what you want!

Sorting It Out

A simple question: What do you *want* Jesus to do for you physically? Ivan Downing illustrates humorously how sorting this out may be difficult. "I had decided to retire from the ministry, and one Sunday I explained my decision to the congregation: 'I wear two hearing aids and tri-focal glasses. I have a partial plate and I sometimes walk with a cane. It seems to me that the Lord is telling me it's time to retire.'"

After the service, a white-haired lady told him, "Reverend, you have misinterpreted what the Lord has been saying to you. He's not telling you it's time to retire. He's telling you that if you keep going, he'll keep you patched up."[2]

Ivan had trouble discerning what he really wanted. Did he really want God to help him adjust to retirement? Or did he really want God's divine health and healing so that he might serve the Lord as long as God enabled him?

Jesus asks you the same penetrating question He asked of the blind beggar: "What do you want me to do for you?" It may be that you have the opportunity right now that the blind man had—Jesus is passing by.

Reflections

1. On a scale of 1 to 10, rate your desire for healing. On the same scale, rate your level of resistance toward your ailment.
2. What do you *want* Jesus to do for you physically?
3. *Why* do you want to be healed?

Prayer

God, I want to be healed physically, not for my own sake, but for Your own pleasure and for Christ's glory. I don't enjoy this sickness. I don't just wish *to be healed, I desperately and persistently* want *to be healed. And I seek a specific healing. I resist this sickness as evil and take my stand against it. Life with this affliction is not life as You intended. I want to be healed.*

Lessons

*What Is God Teaching You
through This Affliction?*

A seed of faith planted by God is now growing in the dark soil of your soul. Before it sprouts into the light of day, a process of deep-down growth is taking place. Perhaps a simple prayer is rising from the depths of your being. The repeated words, *Lord, heal me,* may be increasing in intensity. Yet time may pass before you see your desire fulfilled. What do you do meanwhile?

You place yourself utterly in the hands of God as a learner. You *ask* God to help you learn what He wants to teach you. You *seek* to know God more intimately. You *knock* at the door of heaven to hear a word from God. Like the psalmist, you moan: "My soul thirsts for God, for the living God. When can I go and meet with God?" (Psalm 42:2). During this season of preparation, you are more receptive to God. You are in a learning mode, and the Lord wants to maximize its benefit for you.

Sickness often prompts us to seek beyond ourselves. Pain can serve as God's megaphone to get your attention. As you spend time in Bible reading and reflection, in prayerful meditation, in asking the Lord to apply the Scriptures to you, in waiting upon God in stillness—the divine presence becomes uniquely real. God will speak to you and show you something of Himself.

God Knows What You Need

Years ago a missionary found herself without means among a godless people, far from any source of supplies. She was also in poor health. In her distress she claimed the promise of God that He would supply her need.

One day she received from a businessperson in another part of the country several large boxes of Scotch oatmeal. She already had several cans of condensed milk, so day after day she was obliged to sustain herself with these two commodities. As time went on, this unusual menu seemed to agree with her. After four weeks, she felt in excellent health.

In relating this experience some time later to a group of people, which included a doctor, she was asked more particularly about the nature of her former illness. The physician then said: "The Lord heard your prayer and supplied your need more truly than you realize. For the sickness from which you were suffering, we physicians prescribe a four weeks' diet of nothing but oatmeal gruel for our patients. The Lord prescribed it for you and saw to it that that was all you took. It was the proper remedy."[1]

Yes, God knows exactly what you need and will in His faithfulness make sure you get it. Even when you think you need something else, God will ensure that you receive the one thing you need most.

31

Desiring God Himself

Forgetting your sickness for a while to devote yourself to God alone may be the Lord's prescription. Ultimately, you need God more than you need healing. Taking preliminary steps to know Christ as Savior is of first importance, of course. Then pressing on to know Christ as Sanctifier and Healer and Coming King are other big steps in the spiritual journey.

Beginning at the wrong end does not work. If you want to experience the Lord's touch in your body, then you must know Him and His ways before anything else. Even as important as it is to need and want your healing, which I have already underlined, knowing God is more important. You may have to let go of your healing in order to get God. You may discover that when you have God, you have everything you need.

Friend, the impartation of divine life in your body comes not as an object to be handled, but as a relationship to be experienced. God wants you. God wants you to know Him back. God loves you. God wants you to love Him back. *Do you honestly want God more than anything else, no matter what the outcome?*

Growing Deeper in God's Ways

Sometimes God heals a person quickly at the beginning of his or her spiritual journey. When Chuck, a man in my congregation, came to Christ and received the assurance of salvation, God delivered him immediately from a long habit of cigarette smoking. Yet in the same small church, Anita, an older Christian, continued her struggle with guilt and shame from the same bondage.

Sometimes an older Christian struggles with a sickness, unhealed and unable to understand why. This delay in healing is often a cue that God is leading this beloved child into a deeper experience with Him and into deeper lessons of faith.

Matthew records this conversation after Jesus healed a boy with a demon:

> Then the disciples came to Jesus in private and asked, "Why couldn't we drive it out?" He replied, "Because you have so little faith. I tell you the truth, if you have faith as small as a mustard seed, you can say to this mountain, 'Move from here to there' and it will move. Nothing will be impossible for you."
>
> Matthew 17:19–20

The disciples had previously ministered healing to others in similar predicaments. Here they needed to see how shallow their faith was. What is most encouraging is the striking lesson they then learned about the quality of faith. It was not their energy nor is it ours that removes difficulties. It is God's power. As we draw upon God, authentic faith, not the size of our faith, can accomplish the impossible! Faith is the conduit through which God comes to us.

The pattern for your learning is the same. God may delay answering your prayers to teach you deeper lessons. In this Scripture passage, for example, you learn that mountain-moving faith was not taught to beginners but to Christ's maturing disciples.

I encourage you to deepen your spiritual life through quiet time spent in the Bible, meditation, spiritual reading and prayer. Surrender your life in a new way to God. Why not simply ask: "Lord, what are You trying to teach me? What am I supposed to learn through this? God, how are You inviting me to grow during this chapter of my life? What are You trying to do in my life through this situation?" As you sort these things out before the Lord, listen for His still, small voice.

33

While learning to know God and better understand His ways, you may also learn about yourself. Sickness does not automatically make you more spiritual. But sickness does point out areas in your life that need to be made like Christ. Pain suddenly compels you to get quiet and listen to what God is saying to you. The Lord may reveal ungodly and un-Christlike things about you that you would rather not see. Could it be that you are not quite ready for God to heal you? Perhaps you first need to learn patience or humility.

Sickness is not a virtue, but God can use it to produce virtue within you. The transformation of your character, which you will take into eternity, is more important than the present healing of your body.

Digging Further into Wisdom

Also, as you seek a cure, the larger issues of human suffering may confront you: Why is there evil in the world? Why do the righteous suffer? If God is all-powerful and all-loving, then how can He permit people to suffer? If God is good all the time, then why does He allow birth defects, epidemics, earthquakes, famines and hurricanes? How should individuals, churches and communities respond to the hurts and disappointments of life?

While these issues may come to you, they are really too big for you to wrestle with at this time. I suggest you lay them aside for now. It is enough to acknowledge them, learn what you can learn and lay them aside. Be still and know God (see Psalm 46:10). Keep your pursuit of divine healing simple, childlike, as you come into the presence of Jesus. Healing is a personal intervention of Christ, yes, "a touch" to meet a real need.

This will help you not get sidetracked or discouraged, because even when all the Christian responses to the questions have been given, there are no comfortable answers. Job admitted this to the Lord: "I am unworthy—how can I reply to you? I put my hand over my mouth. I spoke once, but I have no answer—twice, but I will say no more" (Job 40:4–5).

In brief, we can say: God heals today and yet some still suffer. A tension lies between the "already" arrival of God's Kingdom and its "not yet" fulfillment. The admission that "evil is mysterious" is expressed side-by-side with the affirmation that "God is sovereign." As the psalmist recognized, "Our God is in heaven; he does whatever pleases him" (Psalm 115:3).

God is sovereign and His paths are beyond tracing out (see Romans 11:33). The Lord cannot be controlled or manipulated. God may or may not heal. While you hope for healing and while you believe in healing, *God is God whatever the outcome.* The knowledge of God and the transformation of a life are greater than the temporal healing of the body. In any case, God's purposes, whether He heals or not, are always redemptive and transformative. God's grace is sufficient (see 2 Corinthians 12:9).

In the end, even Job did not get an answer for his suffering. He did, however, get a revelation of God. God is sovereign if He heals or does not heal. God's "way is in the whirlwind and the storm, and clouds are the dust of his feet" (Nahum 1:3).

Learning on Both Sides

Barbara Cummisky suffered from multiple sclerosis. For five years she was paralyzed from the waist down. Few of her major organs could function without assistance. She required an oxygen tube in her throat to breathe, was confined to a bed or a wheelchair and constantly fought pain, asthma and pneumonia. She was dying.

35

Then one day as two friends sat with her, a voice told her to walk. She shared this with her friends who helped her get up from the bed. Barbara walked across the room, without an oxygen tube, on legs that had not carried the weight of her body for five years.

Although she had not been out of her house in two years (except for ambulance trips to the hospital), she walked into her church's service that evening. The next day she saw her doctor who invited other doctors to help in testing her thoroughly. No evidence of multiple sclerosis was found. The report of the doctor stated that this was an "obvious answer to prayer and the good hand of God in her life." The doctor then added: "There's no medical explanation. I believe God healed Barbara."[2]

Barbara experienced both the mystery of suffering and the mystery of healing. For five long years she learned the power of a transformed life. In a single moment she learned the power of a divine touch. The life lessons you and I learn in healing or suffering are priceless.

Reflections

1. Do you want God more than anything else, no matter what the outcome?
2. What lessons do you think God may want to teach you during your suffering?
3. What insights are you learning about God, yourself or suffering overall?

Prayer

God, I want to know You more intimately. I want to learn the lessons You mean to teach me. Ultimately, I need You more than I need healing.

I want to know You as Savior, Sanctifier, Healer, Coming King. You are more important than my healing. In this season of waiting, You are becoming more real, and You are showing me things about myself. I am learning about Your power and even deeper lessons of faith and suffering. You are God no matter what the outcome.

4
Scripture

*What Do You Believe
the Bible Says about Healing?*

Another factor you must consider is the theological one. What do you believe the Bible says about healing? You must come to a settled belief that physical healing is in fact taught in the Word of God. The Bible clearly documents and portrays healing as a living truth.

If you believe, for example, that the age of miracles has passed, then you probably will not entertain the notion that healing is possible. You might even resist healing intellectually. Similarly, if you have never personally known someone to be healed, then you might not even consider healing. The idea of God breaking into your world to heal you is beyond your wildest imagination.

Granted, testimonies of others' healing experiences can be useful for bolstering your faith. Stories of God's miraculous intervention to heal others may inspire you to believe that God can do something marvelous for you. But the fulcrum for divine healing is not the testimonies or experiences of others. The real fulcrum of authority is the Bible. God's healing work is found in both Old and New Testament passages. Many seekers overlook references and stories of sickness and healing in the Bible, the very wellspring of our faith. Even if we never saw or heard of any healings whatsoever, we would still believe in healing because the Bible teaches it.

While your personal needs and wants provide the *soil* of faith, the Scriptures provide the *seeds* of faith. You *cultivate* faith through what you need and want, but true faith begins to *rest* on something outside yourself. The assurance of healing is found in the stories and passages, the principles and promises of God's Word.

Your rational mind searches for a foundation upon which to build a sincere faith. You nurture faith through a thorough and honest study of the Scriptures. As you take time to read, meditate on and pray over these Scriptures, the seeds of your faith will germinate.

You may, for example, examine Isaiah 53:4–5 and conclude that Jesus Christ our Great Savior is also our Great Physician:

> Surely he took up our infirmities and carried our sorrows, yet we considered him stricken by God, smitten by him, and afflicted. But he was pierced for our transgressions, he was crushed for our iniquities; the punishment that brought us peace was upon him, and by his wounds we are healed.

According to Isaiah, not only was Jesus "crushed for our iniquities" on the cross but He also took up our "infirmities." The word for *infirmities* is translated as "infirmities" or "sicknesses" (and sometimes "griefs") but is never translated "sin" or "sins." In other words Christ accomplished both goals on the cross: He died for our sins and He bore our physical ailments!

You may also note this statement: He "carried our sorrows." In the original Hebrew, the word *sorrows* literally means our "mental anguish." In fact, Matthew's interpretation of these verses emphasizes healing (see Matthew 8:16–17). Thus, when Jesus died on the cross He provided for our whole being—spiritually, physically and psychologically.

An Army officer consulted a well-known Christian doctor, seeking help for his body and mind. Although his younger years were blessed by the influence of God-fearing parents, he had later thrown aside moral restraint and followed the path of self-indulgence. The harmful effects of such wanton living were evident to the keen spiritual insight of this godly physician.

After examining the soldier, the doctor went to his desk and wrote the following prescription: "Take a portion of Scripture three times daily from the books of the Law, the psalms and the prophets until you are thoroughly convinced of your sin and utter condemnation before God. When this has had its desired effect, receive the words of invitation to accept Christ that are found in the gospels. This will result in a wonderful spiritual change. After your conversion, turn your attention to the book of Acts and the epistles, where you will learn how to enjoy a full life in this world. Finally, when you come to the book of Revelation, it will show you your glorious future in heaven where there will be no further need for prescriptions."

The young officer began to follow the instructions and soon received God's wonderful gift of salvation. As the depression that had overwhelmed him began to lift, his physical condition improved correspondingly. The Word of God had transformed him body, mind and spirit.

Scriptures that are beneficial in forming a healthy theology of healing include the following:

Then Moses cried out to the LORD, and the LORD showed him a piece of wood. He threw it into the water, and the water became sweet. There the LORD made a decree and a law for them, and there he tested them. He said, "If you listen carefully to the voice of the LORD your God and do what is right in his eyes, if you pay attention to his commands and keep all his decrees, I will not bring on you any of the diseases I brought on the Egyptians, for *I am the LORD, who heals you*" (Exodus 15:25–26, emphasis added).	God provides healing before the giving of the Law. God reveals His name and character: "I am the Lord, who heals you."
Praise the LORD, O my soul, and forget not all his benefits—*who forgives all your sins and heals all your diseases*, who redeems your life from the pit and crowns you with love and compassion, who satisfies your desires with good things so that your youth is renewed like the eagle's (Psalm 103:2–5, emphasis added).	God paints a picture of healing after the giving of the Law. God both forgives sins and heals diseases.
Surely *he took up our infirmities* and carried our sorrows, yet we considered him stricken by God, smitten by him, and afflicted. But he was pierced for our transgressions, he was crushed for our iniquities; the punishment that brought us peace was upon him, and *by his wounds we are healed* (Isaiah 53:4–5, emphasis added).	God promises healing before Jesus dies on the cross. Isaiah foretells the Messiah who will bear both sins and sicknesses on the cross.
When evening came, many who were demon-possessed were brought to him, and he drove out the spirits with a word and *healed all the sick*. This was to fulfill what was spoken through the prophet Isaiah: "He took up our infirmities and carried our diseases" (Matthew 8:16–17, emphasis added).	Jesus Christ proclaims healing. Matthew specifically underscores the healing ministry of Jesus as fulfilling the prophecy of Isaiah.
And if the Spirit of him who raised Jesus from the dead is living in you, he who raised Christ from the dead *will also give life to your mortal bodies* through his Spirit, who lives in you (Romans 8:11, emphasis added).	Paul pronounces healing through the resurrected Christ. The same Holy Spirit who raised Jesus from the dead gives life to our mortal bodies.

41

"Everything is permissible for me"—but not everything is beneficial. "Everything is permissible for me"—but I will not be mastered by anything. "Food for the stomach and the stomach for food"—but God will destroy them both. *The body is* not meant for sexual immorality, but *for the Lord, and the Lord for the body* (1 Corinthians 6:12–13, emphasis added).	Paul pledges healing through our union with Christ. Not only are our bodies for the Lord, but the Lord is for our bodies.
Is any one of you in trouble? He should pray. Is anyone happy? Let him sing songs of praise. Is any one of you sick? *He should call the elders of the church to pray over him and anoint him with oil in the name of the Lord. And the prayer offered in faith will make the sick person well; the Lord will raise him up.* If he has sinned, he will be forgiven. Therefore confess your sins to each other and pray for each other so that you may be healed. The prayer of a righteous man is powerful and effective (James 5:13–16, emphasis added).	James presents the healing ministry of the local church. The church is to practice healing.
He himself bore our sins in his body on the tree, so that we might die to sins and live for righteousness; *by his wounds you have been healed* (1 Peter 2:24).	God provides healing through the cross. Christ's death provides physical healing and healing from the sickness of sin.

After reflecting on these passages, you may conclude that God makes provision in the redemptive work of the Lord Jesus Christ for the healing of our physical bodies. Furthermore, praying for the sick is the privilege of the Church in this present age. For further study, see Appendix 1: "The Healing Ministry of Jesus Christ in the Gospels." With English poet, hymn writer and theologian Frederick Faber (1814–1863), you may celebrate God's mercy: "There is healing in His blood."[1]

Pinpointing Your Beliefs

In order to help you pinpoint how you view God in relation to healing, I recommend you review the following ten-point scale. The theological question is this: Can and does God heal? If so, on what basis? As you consider these various statements, try to discern where you find yourself and your own faith development.

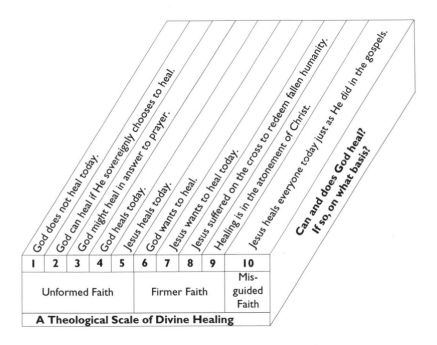

A Theological Scale of Divine Healing

1. *"God does not heal today."* People who state this may be fully convinced that God healed in Bible times or that Jesus healed to prove His deity. Nevertheless, they are theologically or culturally hemmed in from accepting the reality of healing today. They reason that we must accept sickness. To them we will only realize complete healing after this life or when Christ comes again. Some are afraid of reli-

43

gious fanaticism. Their trust is primarily in doctors, science and medicine.

2. *"God can heal if He sovereignly chooses to heal."* Some people believe that asking for healing presumes on God's sovereignty. They say that God *can* heal because He is powerful and that God can choose to suspend the laws of nature. They conclude, however, that most often God withholds healing and that healing is rare. They may not believe that personalized prayer will make any fundamental difference that results in healing. They may say, "God can heal, but He probably won't. Prayer may work but probably not." Or, "Prayer may help but mostly to give God's peace and presence in suffering." Their belief in God's sovereignty is out of balance with God's nearness and desire to work in someone's life.

3. *"God might heal in answer to prayer."* People who think this way take healing a step further. They believe that prayer might make a difference, but they are also full of doubts. They may see a physical affliction as a call to prayer, to draw closer to God. In other words, they believe that prayer certainly will not hurt, and it may indeed in a general way help someone feel better. The full idea of healing, however, is still distant.

4. *"God heals today."* Frequently when people think of the needs of others, perhaps those distant from themselves, they can affirm that God heals today. But suddenly when they themselves are suffering, they discover that this kind of indistinct faith is less satisfying. It is a step forward, but it still does not go far enough personally.

5. *"Jesus heals today."* The belief in the uniqueness of the incarnation of Jesus Christ moves people a further step toward healing. Those who see the ex-

44

alted, majestic God revealed in Jesus are affirming that God is also close and personal. If God broke into time and space to show us His character more fully, then we can more clearly see His ways and desires in the healing activity of Christ as recorded in the gospels. God is brought near to us in Christ. This is a helpful step. Still, their theological faith is not distinct and not personalized.

6. *"God wants to heal."* Others conclude that the Bible teaches about healing and expresses God's will to heal. Their faith focus begins to move from their heads to their hearts. They may emphasize that God's desire to heal is an expression of His mercy and compassion. "Healing is something God *wants* to do," they say. This heightened awareness of God's desire to heal brings them in a new arena of faith. They view their potential healing as being initiated by God. I see this as a significant step forward.

7. *"Jesus wants to heal today."* Faith begins to take a sharper focus when people conclude that the same incarnate Jesus who healed while on earth in the first century is the same risen and ascended Lord Jesus who is alive today and still heals today. They believe that Jesus responds in mercy and compassion to suffering humanity and acts with power to heal. They understand theologically that this Scripture, "Jesus Christ is the same yesterday and today and forever" (Hebrews 13:8), includes healing.

8. *"Jesus suffered on the cross to redeem fallen humanity."* Faith continues to peak when people believe that healing is possible because of the redemptive work of Jesus' shed blood. These believers affirm that access to wholeness for body, mind and spirit is rooted in the fact that Jesus took up our infirmities as well as our sins on the cross. They maintain that God is utterly sovereign—He can say no. Yet

45

they equally believe that our infirmities have been dealt with by Jesus' death.

9. *"Healing is in the atonement of Christ."* Other Christians also see a connection between the atonement and healing. They maintain that Jesus died and rose again to redeem our physical bodies in need of healing. They do not, however, go so far as to say that healing is available to the same degree that salvation is. They believe that "everyone who calls on the name of the Lord will be saved" (Romans 10:13), but they do not believe that everyone who calls on the name of the Lord will be healed. They see healing as a privilege for believers—but not something that they can demand.

10. *"Jesus heals everyone today just as He did in the gospels."* Some Christians maintain that the Bible guarantees healing and that faith compels God to act. Notice the word *compels*. God's sovereignty is set aside in the demands made on Him for healing. They assert that healing is provided in the atonement just as salvation is, and that we, therefore, have a "right" to it. If a sick person is not healed, these individuals are quick to assume that the cause is either unconfessed sin or a lack of faith.

Where are you on this theological scale of divine healing? Do you find yourself stuck or growing? My supposition is that those who find themselves theologically within numbers 6 through 9 are more likely to encounter the Lord in healing. Their faith has found a *firmer* resting place in God's Word. Those whose theology of healing is on the lower end of this scale, between 1 and 5, may less likely experience healing. They have an *unformed* theology of healing. I think those who hold to number 10 have gone too far on the theological scale.

Their faith, though sincere, is *misguided* and can cling to false hopes.

Will God heal someone who does not believe that healing is in the atonement? Can God work in the life and body of someone whose faith is weak and *unformed*? Yes, because God is God and He can do whatever He wishes.

From the other side of the scale, we have to ask, Does God heal even when people have *misguided* faith, which is fraught with theological and spiritual dangers? Again, yes, because God responds to faith, and He works within His people to correct their misguided emphases.

Still, Scripture shows that God most often responds to someone's *firm* faith. This has been my experience as well.

Even though I believe that healing is in the atonement, I know that not all Christians will agree with me. That's okay. At a later stage, I will encourage you to listen to the Lord to give you a specific passage upon which to rest your faith—to receive a word from the Lord for you. A single promise of the Scriptures is enough if you really grasp it, even if you do not see healing in the atonement. At this stage of your faith development, settling your belief that the Bible teaches physical healing is enough.

Albert Simpson (1843–1919), founder of The Christian and Missionary Alliance, affirmed:

> There is healing in the promise,
> There is healing in the blood,
> There is strength for all our weakness
> In the risen Son of God.[2]

Maturing in Both Head and Heart

Your theological development is entwined with your faith development, which frequently progresses in stages. Under the stress of affliction, your intellectual knowledge of correct doctrine can lead to an inner knowing of truth. Also included in this cognitive, theological search is greater submission to the authority of God's Word and God's will. These combinations are essential for nurturing the highest faith and leading into the fullest experience of healing. In brief, God wants you to mature in both your head and your heart!

Let me illustrate. You may have already exercised faith in the Lord Jesus to *save* you. "God our Savior . . . wants all . . . to be saved and to come to a knowledge of the truth" (1 Timothy 2:3–4). You may have also experienced a deeper work of the Holy Spirit to *fill* you and make you *holy*. "It is God's will that you should be sanctified" (1 Thessalonians 4:3). Perhaps you are now at a stage in your faith development to experience the Lord God as your *healer*. You may identify with the man with leprosy: "Lord, if you are willing, you can make me clean." Likewise, you may envision Jesus reaching out His hand to touch you, saying, "I am willing. . . . Be clean!" (Matthew 8:2–3).

What is my point? The texts of Scripture provide the basis for you to believe that God will save you, fill you, sanctify you *and* heal you. Through the texts of Scripture you learn that God is concerned for your physical well-being. Through the texts of Scripture you find the assurance of an infusion of the life of the Lord Jesus Christ in your physical body. Augustine (354–430), Bishop of Hippo, said, "I never have any difficulty believing in miracles, since I experienced the miracle of a change in my own heart."[3]

I can point the way, but you must follow the path to pray over specific passages of God's Word until you know in your head and feel in your heart what God wants for you. *A biblical theology of healing is the basis for receiving a specific word from the Lord for your healing.*

The Holy Spirit Will Guide You

Let me make all this heady stuff practical. How often have you found yourself in the same situation as the father whose son was under the control of a demon?

> Jesus asked the boy's father, "How long has he been like this?" "From childhood," he answered. "It has often thrown him into fire or water to kill him. But if you can do anything, take pity on us and help us." "'If you can'?" said Jesus. "Everything is possible for him who believes." Immediately the boy's father exclaimed, "I do believe; help me overcome my unbelief!"
>
> Mark 9:21–24

Quoting from the man's own words, Jesus asked, "'If you can'?" Even in the depths of your despair and weakness, Jesus is stirring you to new faith. He is calling something of true faith to emerge from the depths of your being, for "everything is possible for him who believes."

There is a great difference between the *scathing rebuke* Jesus earlier gave to His disciples as part of an "unbelieving generation" and the *gentle chiding* with which Jesus addressed this troubled father. It was a matter of tone. The tone of Jesus' voice here was not sarcastic snippiness, "If you can!" His voice was quiet but firm, gentle but unbending, "'If you can'?" In this gentle chiding, Jesus stirred this father to authentic faith.

A frog found himself caught in a deep rut on a country road. His friends tried to help him get out, but their efforts were in vain. At last in great sadness they left him. But the very next day one of these friends was hopping along that country road, and whom did he meet but the same frog who the day before had been hopelessly stuck in the rut.

49

The frog was joyful and very pleased with himself. Astonished, the friend asked: "How did you get free? I thought you were stuck for good and couldn't get out!" The freed frog said: "That's right, I couldn't. But a truck started coming along that rut toward me, and I *had* to get out!" That is just the kind of nudge God sometimes gives us! We *have* to get out of the rut, so in a crisis we activate our faith and call out to God!

But frankly our faith is often weak. Have you felt like the father in this story—one moment saying, "I do believe," and the next moment saying, "Help me overcome my unbelief!"? This parent had been disappointed too often. He was doing his best to have faith but he was also honest enough to admit his doubts. The heartbreak of tragedy often brings us to our knees in total dependence upon God. We finally admit: "Unless God does something, nothing will happen. Unless the Lord intervenes, my child will not get better. Unless the Spirit of God steps in, my situation will not change."

So we burst out in faith with a cry for more faith: "God, do something! Intervene. Step in. Change me. Touch my loved one. Redeem this situation. I do believe, but my faith is weak. Overcome my unbelief. I *have* faith. But help me where it fails. Take away my doubt and discouragement. Fill me full of faith. I need a miracle."

Be assured—the Holy Spirit "will guide you into all truth" (John 16:13), including the truth about healing.

Reflections

1. What do you believe the Bible says about healing? What specific Scriptures would you include in developing a theology of healing?
2. Where are you on the ten-point theological scale of divine healing?

3. Where are you affirming, "I do believe," and where are you crying out, "Help me overcome my unbelief!"?

Prayer

God, what does Your Word teach about healing? My faith is looking for a resting place in the Word, not just someone else's experience to lean on. Guide me as I search the Scriptures. Can You and do You heal today? If so, on what basis? Spirit of God, please guide me into all truth, including the truth about healing.

5
Love

Does God Really Love You?

J udy Balswick was fourteen and a new believer. She
had developed a painful infection in her foot due to
a splinter that had been embedded in it for years.
When a Christian girlfriend asked if she had prayed for
healing, Judy admitted that she had not even thought
about that. Though Judy was a bit skeptical, her friend
gathered a group of Christian friends around her to pray
for her foot to be healed.

As Judy stood there in the center of that little group,
God used their faith to encourage her. When she woke
up the next morning, the infection was oozing, an indica-
tion that it was starting to clear up. Eventually the small
piece of wood worked its way out and got stuck to the
bandage. Through this experience God taught her as a
young Christian that Jesus really cared about her personally. Her friends had pointed her to Jesus as her Healer,
and her faith was strengthened.[1] The Lord often uses other
people to express His love and concern.

The ability to receive any gift from God can often be
traced to the capacity to receive God's love. Being persuaded that "God is love" (1 John 4:8, 16) is not enough.

God's love needs to be personalized: "God loves *me*. Not only did Jesus die on the cross for the whole world, He died for *me*. The Holy Spirit empowers and counsels *me*. *I* am God's beloved child. The Lord can be depended upon to hear and answer *my* prayer."

Living in negativity can breed a deep sense of anxiety, inferiority and self-doubt. These can make it difficult for you to embrace the belief that God accepts you fully and loves you as a person just the way you are. These feelings can limit your full expression of faith to receive.

You may feel unworthy to receive healing. You may think that you are not good enough to deserve God's gift to you. You may feel spiritually weak to claim any of God's specific mercies. You may be inwardly struggling: "Does God really love me? Why would God want to heal me? How can God care for me unconditionally?" You might conclude: "If God really knew me, He would reject me. God might heal others, but not *me*."

Being convinced of God's personal love for you is an important factor in experiencing His healing. A basic prerequisite for receiving healing is the assurance of an all-loving and completely dependable God. *Let me encourage you—God will gently lead you to know that He loves you and wants to heal you!* In fact, while you are seeking healing, the attribute of God's love may seem to crest even higher than His sovereign power or His mysterious ways. The Lord's display of His mighty power in your body will then be a further demonstration of His wonderful love.

Receiving the Father's Love

A key to receiving God the Father's love is affirming what He said about you in His Word. When you affirm

His Word, you are saying: "I believe what God says. I believe what God says about me."

Following is a series of affirmations and verses that work for me concerning God's love. I have a copy of these verses in my Bible. Periodically I pull out this list and review it to affirm the simple truth of Scripture that *God loves me.*

God Loves Me

But because of *his great love for us,* God, who is rich in mercy, made us alive with Christ even when we were dead in transgressions—it is by grace you have been saved.

Ephesians 2:4–5, emphasis added

God Showed His Love to Me

This is love: not that we loved God, but that *he loved us* and sent his Son as an atoning sacrifice for our sins. Dear friends, since *God so loved us,* we also ought to love one another.

1 John 4:10–11, emphasis added

God Is My Heavenly Father

For you did not receive a spirit that makes you a slave again to fear, but you received the Spirit of sonship. And by him we cry, *"Abba, Father."*

Romans 8:15, emphasis added

I Am God's Beloved Child

Be imitators of God, therefore, as *dearly loved children.* . . .

Ephesians 5:1, emphasis added

God Says to Me, "I Love You"

Since you are precious and honored in my sight, and because *I love you* . . .

Isaiah 43:4, emphasis added

Nothing Will Separate Me from God's Love

Neither height nor depth, *nor anything* else in all creation, *will be able to separate us from the love of God* that is in Christ Jesus our Lord.

Romans 8:39, emphasis added

God Delights in Me

"The LORD your God is with you, he is mighty to save. *He will take great delight in you*, he will quiet you with his love, he will rejoice over you with singing."

Zephaniah 3:17, emphasis added

God Loves Me in Spite of Everything

The LORD is compassionate and gracious, slow to anger, abounding in love. He will not always accuse, nor will he harbor his anger forever; he does not treat us as our sins deserve or repay us according to our iniquities. For as high as the heavens are above the earth, *so great is his love for those who fear him*; as far as the east is from the west, so far has he removed our transgressions from us. As a father has compassion on his children, so *the LORD has compassion on those who fear him*; for he knows how we are formed, he remembers that we are dust.

Psalm 103:8–14, emphasis added

As you open your heart to receive the Father's love, He will come to you. *God will reveal His love to you where you need it most.* The Lord will grant you a divine encounter.

With unconditional love, He will revolutionize your life and your relationship with Him. The Holy Spirit will help you, guide you, draw you and teach you to receive God's love and to know God as your heavenly Father.

How very different Christian healing is from the illusion of sickness expressed in Christian Science or the impersonal force in Buddhism! We can know and experience the God of the Bible. We have an intimate relationship with God through Jesus Christ. And through a personal encounter with the living God, we also experience the power of His love in divine healing.

Seeing Jesus Love the Sick

In the gospels we read consistently of Christ's compassion for the sick. When He walked on the earth Jesus touched those who had not been touched *in years*—those with decaying flesh, ears clogged with years of deafness, eyes caked with disease, running sores, bleeding wounds, deformed limbs. He touched them all. One compelling example is Jesus' approach to the man with leprosy:

> A man with leprosy came to him and begged him on his knees, "If you are willing, you can make me clean." Filled with compassion, Jesus reached out his hand and touched the man. "I am willing," he said. "Be clean!" Immediately the leprosy left him and he was cured.
>
> Mark 1:40–42

Jesus loves the unlovely and touches the untouchable. He forgives the foul, saves the sinner and heals the hideous. For this disfigured leper, Jesus reached out in compassion and extended His power to heal.

To express love and acceptance with our eyes is one thing. To express love and acceptance with a touch is quite another. The touch of Jesus often released His power but first it was a sign of God's compassionate care. His touch soothed. His touch revealed His desire to help. His touch then displayed His power to heal.

In this way His touch goes deeper than physical healing. Jesus touches the inner person, the real you. With a *touch* comes His presence, His identification, His affirmation, His security, His affection. Jesus *sees* you in your need. He *looks* into your soul and accepts you as you are. And He extends His hand and *touches* you at your greatest need. Yes, because Jesus still loves the sick, He still heals the sick.

Reflections

1. Does God really love you and want to heal you?
2. What does God say about you in the Bible?
3. Can you imagine Jesus reaching out to touch you in your need?

Prayer

> *God, sometimes I wonder: Do You really love me? Why would You want to heal me? Yet I know that You are an all-loving and completely dependable God. I know in my head that You accept and love me just the way I am, although sometimes I feel unworthy. I don't feel good enough to deserve or claim any of Your specific mercies. Yet I am gradually becoming convinced in my heart that You love me and that You want to heal me. Grant me the grace to experience Your love where I need it most. Touch me and heal me, Savior divine!*

57

6

Faith

Will God Heal You and Heal You at This Time?

Imagine yourself walking out gradually into a lake or an ocean. With every step, you are going deeper into the water and the water is rising higher on your body. That is a good image of deepening faith. With every step, you are going deeper and the water is rising higher. The deeper you go into God's Word and God's Spirit, the more you become immersed in the possibility of God's action for you.[1]

So far we have looked at what you *need* and *want* from God. We examined things to be learned—both *personal lessons* and a *biblical understanding*. Then we explored the capacity to receive *God's love* in a tangible way.

Now I want you to consider applying these principles of physical healing to your particular need at this particular time. The revelation of God concerning healing may still feel outside you; it is time to go further in applying God's Word to your current experience.

As you enter deeper waters, you find that the external Word of God has personal application. The written Word becomes a specific word for you. The broad promises for all people and all times become a special assurance for you in this present moment.

By now you no longer wonder *if* God can heal. You freely admit that Christ has the power to heal. The practical questions emerging from your heart at this stage are more personal and pointed: Will God heal *me*? Will God heal me *at this time*?

Having Faith in God

If you could surgically remove your faith so you could examine its condition, it might look rather limp. That would not be very helpful. Let me remind you of the *object* of your faith, for Jesus said, "Have faith in *God*" (Mark 11:22, emphasis added).

I am convinced that the Holy Spirit will lead you to become more and more persuaded that this God—the Creator of all things, the Sovereign Lord, the Omnipotent One, the Almighty—will break into your world and meet your particular need in the present now! God wants you to see Him as He is, and the Holy Spirit will nurture that heavenly vision and bring into fulfillment all that He has for you.

This same Lord Jesus who was born a baby, lived on earth, ministered in love and power, died on the cross, rose from the dead, ascended into heaven and lives forevermore will enter your situation and make you whole. This "Jesus Christ is the same yesterday and today and forever" (Hebrews 13:8). This is the God in whom you are placing your trust! This is the vision of Jesus that Albert Simpson put into words:

> Oft on earth He healed the sufferer
> By His mighty hand;
> Still our sicknesses and sorrows
> Go at His command.

59

He who gave His healing virtue
To a woman's touch,
To the faith that claims His fullness
Still will give as much.[2]

Even the hope that God wants you whole may be just the evidence that true faith has germinated in you and is starting to grow. Something of God is stirring within you. The inner movements of God are at work drawing you to receive. That is the Holy Spirit working. That is the dawn and rising of faith. Your faith in God is what He wants.

You see, friend, there is a great difference between having faith *in faith* and having faith *in God*. Jesus said, "Have faith in God" (Mark 11:22). If faith were something you could muster within yourself, it would not last. It would melt away like dew in the rising sun. In fact, if you try extracting your faith to see how it is growing, it will die! Look not at your faith but at the object of your faith.

How do you know the difference between having faith *in faith* and having faith *in God*? Having faith in faith is trying to force God's hand to act. But God's hand cannot be forced. Having faith in faith is trying to manipulate God's will. But God's will cannot be manipulated. Having faith in faith is trying to manufacture faith by working up some supreme inner confidence in God. But faith is not working up some emotion, nor are miracles the result of positive thinking or believing really hard.

Nor will following all the steps in this book guarantee healing, *unless something of God is being birthed in you.* When God is at work, you will know it. Your faith born from above will grow and develop and come to fruition. As true faith matures, God's love is released in powerful ways to touch body, mind and spirit.

This is the fundamental difference between *faith* healing and *divine* healing. Yes, faith is an important component for healing, but it is always faith in God. You do not seek a heightened state of consciousness. Nor do you work up some intense emotion. Nor do you need an elevated state of mind. These are all expressions of what true faith is not. Faith in itself has no inherent power to cure anybody. Nor will placing your hope in some dynamic faith healer make the difference.

The real source of power in divine healing is the Lord of heaven and earth, the God of the Bible, the personal God who fully revealed Himself in Jesus Christ. It is this God in whom you are putting your trust! When you have faith in faith, the direction of your gaze is *inward*. When you have faith in God, the direction is *upward*.

Believing God Can

Faith believes God can. Faith believes God has the power. Dudley Woodberry recounts an incident in Nigeria where a Muslim man paid a local shaman to curse a group of Christians who were evangelizing so they would die. But the Muslim man got sick instead, and the shaman could not lift the spell. In desperation the Muslim asked the Christians—the very ones he tried to curse—to pray for him. They did and he was delivered. Realizing where true power came from, the Muslim became a follower of Jesus Christ.[3] Faith believes God has the power.

Faith also sees God as He is. Faith believes what God can do. Faith anticipates what God will do. Healing may come when your vision of God is finally greater than your own need. Matthew told how two blind men came to Jesus for healing:

As Jesus went on from there, two blind men followed him, calling out, "Have mercy on us, Son of David!" When he had gone indoors, the blind men came to him, and he asked them, "Do you believe that I am able to do this?" "Yes, Lord," they replied. Then he touched their eyes and said, "According to your faith will it be done to you"; and their sight was restored.

Matthew 9:27–30

It almost seems a little mean for these two blind men to have to follow Jesus around—groping their way eventually into a house. Yet Jesus was testing their tenacity and persistence. Did they really want to be healed? Besides, He wanted to deal with them apart from the crowd, even as you must face God alone for your own need.

Jesus also wanted to be satisfied that their faith was real. "Do you believe that I am able to do this?" Was their faith worked up from within or was it truly born from above? With two words they affirmed Christ's identity (earlier they had addressed Him as "Son of David") and confessed their faith in Him: "Yes, Lord." This dual admission released God's power for their healing. Their faith in God was genuine.

Essentially Jesus said to them: "You want it? You got it! Are you willing to chase it a little? Then you win! Let it happen, then, just as you believe!" According to their faith it was done to them, and their sight was restored.

These blind men believed what Jesus could do *for them*. The way to receive your miracle is to place yourself utterly in the hands of Jesus Christ and begin saying: "I know what You can do, Lord. Only do it, and do it for me."

Gregory of Nyssa (ca. 330–395), Cappadocian bishop, one of the four great Eastern Fathers and champion of orthodoxy, recorded how God healed the young daughter of a soldier who was blind. The membranes around her pupils were swollen and whitened by disease. Macrina (ca. 327–380), the elder sister of both Basil the Great and Gregory of Nyssa, announced prophetically that the miracle-working power of Christ would heal this girl: "I have some medicine which is especially effective in curing eye diseases."

Later the little girl's nurse saw that she was healed and said: "Nothing of what was promised to us has been omitted, but the true medicine that heals diseases, the cure that comes from prayer, this she has given us, and it has already worked; nothing at all is left of the disease of the eyes." Then the overwhelmed father said:

> As she said this, she took our child and put her in my arms and I, also, then comprehended the miracles in the gospel which I had not believed before and I said: "What a great thing it is for sight to be restored to the blind by the hand of God, if now His handmaiden makes such cures and has done such a thing through faith in Him, a fact no less impressive than these miracles."[4]

Let your faith look up to God.

Reflections

1. As you are seeking healing, as best as you can, describe the inner movements of God.
2. What is the primary focal point of your faith?
3. What are you doing with the faith you have?

Prayer

God, I am wondering if You will heal me. Will You heal me at this time? I know You have the

63

power. Yet I need to be persuaded that You will meet my particular need at this time. As I read the written Word of God, my faith is growing because I see who You are. I am learning to move beyond having faith in faith *that comes from looking inward and having faith* in God *that comes from looking upward. I know what You can do, Lord. Only do it, do it for me and do it at this time. My faith looks up to You.*

7

Cause

What Is the Underlying Cause of Your Sickness?

In giving advice to marathon runners, Joe Henderson, a columnist for *Runner's World*, recommends that for every mile they run in a competitive race, they take a day off from regular training. He maintains: "Runners make the incorrect assumption that once the soreness in muscles is gone, then they are recovered. But thousands of microscopic tears in the muscles can take four to six weeks for complete healing."[1]

While playing sports most people work muscles that they do not normally use. The result is soreness and tiredness. Unless they acknowledge the underlying muscle tears and take time for the remedy—rest and relaxation—they may face greater problems later.

Likewise as your faith in the Lord for healing grows, you will need to look at the underlying root cause of your illness. Most people want to know the reason for problems. Americans in particular think that if they discover and remove the cause of some concern, they will resolve the problem. Medically, of course, this approach has great benefit. If you remove a sliver from your finger, then the discomfort will ease and healing can take place.

Indeed, discerning the cause can be crucial to finding a cure, for an underlying cause may have direct impact on a physical illness. Yet, like medicine, similar symptoms can have a variety of underlying causes. An illness may stem from any of these:

- Physiological disease
- Psychological disorder
- Mental illness
- Emotional hurt
- Mental habit
- Personal or family sin
- Divine discipline or action
- Demonic influence or activity
- Accident
- Work-related injury
- Birth defect
- Old age
- Abuse to the body
- Improper diet
- Inadequate exercise

Discerning the cause can help guide your praying.

Confronting the Cause

The way to handle a physical problem caused by unresolved guilt, anger or resentment would be different from dealing with a condition caused by an accident. At this point, ask God to search your heart. Ask the Lord to deal gently with anything in you that might not be right before Him. King David prayed: "Search me, O God, and know my heart; test me and know my anxious thoughts. See if there is any offensive way in me, and lead me in the way everlasting" (Psalm 139:23–24).

The relationship between our minds and bodies or between our spiritual and physical natures needs to be taken into account. When we fill our hearts with praise, joy and gratitude, for instance, our whole being often feels better. On the other hand, when we have become discouraged, gloomy and sour, we frequently feel worn out and tired. Someone said, "Cheerful people resist disease better than glum ones. In other words, the surly bird catches the germ."[2]

As you pray, you may learn that your failure to forgive someone is the real cause of your physical problem. Or the Lord may convict you of an unhealthy habit. Or you may come to a place of acceptance that some aches and pains are part of growing older, though God can give you grace to face them all. Or you may conclude that your condition has happened through no fault of your own and you just need God's mercy.

Direction for Prayer

Do you see how discerning the underlying cause of your illness is important? God wants to heal your whole person. Brother Lawrence (ca. 1614–1691), a French Christian mystic and Carmelite lay brother, said, "God is often (in some sense) nearer to us, and more effectually present with us, in sickness than in health. . . . He often sends diseases of the body to cure those of the soul. Comfort yourself with the sovereign Physician of both the soul and the body."[3]

If this area is too difficult for you to sort through, seek the advice of a mature Christian or the counsel of your pastor. Be open to their directives. Or ask God to guide you to discern the cause. Once properly discerned through prayer and counsel, an underlying cause may need to be dealt with before anything else.

Knowing the cause of your sickness is often an important step. *The cause may signal what specific strategy to take in prayer toward divine healing.*

In brief, if a sickness is caused by sin, then repentance is imperative. If an illness or physical problem stems from past emotional hurts, then forgiveness is required. If a physical problem is the result of physical damage or a physical disorder or malfunction, then prayer for restoration or adjustment of whatever is causing the problem is called for. If an ailment is provoked by demonic activity, then the evil powers behind the presenting condition need to be confronted in Jesus' name. If God has revealed that someone is sick with a sickness unto death, then prayer for peace and grace for the loved one, family and friends is fitting.[4]

Let's look more closely at two of the root causes from the list above—sin and demonic activity—to show scriptural precedent for discernment and not jumping to conclusions too quickly.

Sin and Sickness

Some well-meaning Christians point their fingers at sick people and say, "The reason that person is sick is because of sin in his or her life." Some might have pointed their accusing fingers at you and declared you "Guilty!" This is the same accusation Job's so-called comforters gave. They wrongly believed that suffering is always due to personal sin or disobedience to God.

Yet, while acknowledging that not all physical problems are the result of sin, we must admit that some are.

The man at the pool of Bethesda is a good example. He had been an invalid for 38 years and then Jesus dramatically healed him and gave him a direct challenge: "Get up! Pick up your mat and walk." John then reports, "At once the man was cured; he picked up his mat and walked" (John 5:8–9).

John concludes this story with a probable cause for his illness: "Later Jesus found him at the temple and said to him, 'See, you are well again. *Stop sinning* or something worse may happen to you'" (John 5:14, emphasis added).

Jesus implied that this man's former condition was a direct result of sin. Something worse might happen if he continued his self-destructive ways. Apparently he had been lax in thinking about sin. He had not confessed his sin and it had destroyed him for 38 years. He needed the stimulus of this warning to keep his healing. He had brought this affliction upon himself.

Later Jesus would reject the notion that all physical suffering was caused by sin:

> As he went along, he saw a man blind from birth. His disciples asked him, "Rabbi, who sinned, this man or his parents, that he was born blind?" "Neither this man nor his parents sinned," said Jesus, "but this happened so that the work of God might be displayed in his life."
>
> John 9:1–3

In other words, sin can cause sickness, but not all sickness is caused by sin.

Demonic Attack and Sickness

Similarly, evil spirits sometimes afflict people's bodies but we cannot declare that all crippled people have become subject to demon spirits. Similar afflictions can have different causes.

In the gospels, for instance, we read of two men who both struggled with an inability to talk. Yet Jesus detected different underlying causes and dealt with each accordingly.

> There some people brought to him a man who was deaf and could hardly talk, and they begged him to place his hand on the man. After he took him aside, away from the crowd, Jesus put his fingers into the man's ears. Then he spit and touched the man's tongue. He looked up to heaven and with a deep sigh said to him, *"Ephphatha!"* (which means, "Be opened!"). At this, the man's ears were opened, his tongue was loosened and he began to speak plainly.
>
> Mark 7:32–35

> While they were going out, a man who was demon-possessed and could not talk was brought to Jesus. And when the demon was driven out, the man who had been mute spoke. The crowd was amazed and said, "Nothing like this has ever been seen in Israel."
>
> Matthew 9:32–33

The symptoms or manifestations appeared similar—they both could not talk—but the causes were different. Jesus healed one of a physical affliction and delivered the other from a demon.

This shows the importance of discernment in dealing with any sickness. We might, for instance, need to discern between mental illness caused by emotional wounds and behavior caused by demon spirits. A mentally ill person and a demonically controlled person may experience similar conditions, yet one requires counseling and prayer for healing; the other counseling and prayer for deliverance.

Likewise, we do not label a neurological or hormonal problem or chemical imbalance as a demon problem and vice versa.

Regarding the question of demonic attack, let me add that we dare not look for a demon under every rock, but we also dare not bury our heads in the sand when demonic activity is really the underlying cause. Here is some pastoral advice: Look for the demonic cause last, not first. Whatever the cause, Hilary of Poitiers (ca. 315–367), a French bishop and vigorous defender of Christian orthodoxy, declared: "We become steadfast in hope and receive the gifts of healing. Demons are made subject to our authority."[5]

A Case Study

Sor Thao and her husband, Vue, Hmong immigrants from Southeast Asia, live in Michigan in a close-knit community. Sor had been sick for a month and was having difficulty keeping her food down. Her husband had taken her to the hospital emergency room several times, but the doctors could not determine the source of her problem and medication they prescribed was not helping.

Vue's father, Cher Jor, who was not a believer, had forbidden Vue and Sor to be baptized, because he was afraid they would abandon the family's religious rituals. Cher Jor called the extended family together and directed a shaman to perform healing rituals for Sor. When Sor continued to worsen, Cher Jor finally gave them permission to pray to their God, saying: "Let the Christians try. If Sor is healed, then the family may be baptized."

That night other Christians from their church gathered in Vue and Sor's apartment, surrounded by the

71

couple's non-Christian family members, to pray and sing praise. Their pastor, Shua Cha, presented the Gospel and Vue, Sor and their five children knelt to acknowledge their faith in Jesus publicly. Pastor Shua pressed the issue, asking if they were willing to forsake the old ways. They said they were.

Then the pastor asked for a pair of scissors and cut off the white strings the shaman had tied around Sor's arms as prayers to evil spirits. Other items that were signs of the old ways were also cleaned out and placed in an open Bible.

After leading them in prayer, Pastor Shua divided the Christians present into small groups. They prayed in every room of the apartment, asking God to cast out the evil spirits. After prayer, the items of the old ways were taken out and burned (see Acts 19:19).

As the Christians continued to pray daily, gradually Sor got better, and the entire family was baptized a month later.[6] Praise the Lord!

This story shows that dramatic results can come when the underlying cause of sickness is dealt with. The root problem may not always be this evident, but if finding it is a factor in your healing, the Lord will help you determine what it is.

Keeping the Right Focus

We see that finding the cause of sickness may well be an important step toward healing, but we also need to guard against excessive focus in this area. In Jesus' ministry, there were times that the cause of sickness did not seem to make much difference to Him: He healed all who came to Him. His healing power *dealt with* the source of each person's malady, but He did not necessarily *disclose* that source:

He went down with them and stood on a level place. A large crowd of his disciples was there and a great number of people from all over Judea, from Jerusalem, and from the coast of Tyre and Sidon, who had come to hear him and to be healed of their diseases. Those troubled by evil spirits were cured, and the people all tried to touch him, because power was coming from him and healing them all.

Luke 6:17–19

When evening came, many who were demon-possessed were brought to him, and he drove out the spirits with a word and healed all the sick.

Matthew 8:16

Many followed him, and he healed all their sick.

Matthew 12:15

And when the men of that place recognized Jesus, they sent word to all the surrounding country. People brought all their sick to him and begged him to let the sick just touch the edge of his cloak, and all who touched him were healed.

Matthew 14:35–36

It is interesting to note that on some occasions, as with those listed above, Jesus and the disciples healed *all* the sick (see also Matthew 4:23–24; 10:1; 15:30; Mark 6:56; Luke 4:40). On other occasions Jesus healed *many* (see Mark 1:32–34; 3:10; 6:13; Luke 7:21) or *not many* (see Matthew 13:58).

No doubt Jesus encountered people whom He did not heal. He apparently walked by many sick people to show His power to the man at the pool of Bethesda (see John 5:2–3). We are left to wonder if Jesus may have deepened the faith of those whom He left in their

73

infirmities. Perhaps others who saw Christ later trusted Him as their Savior and Healer. This may have been the case with the crippled beggar at the Temple whom He healed through the ministry of Peter and John (see Acts 3:1–10).

In any case, the point is this: *Your focus should not be on the cause of your illness but on Jesus.* It is Jesus who healed then and heals today.

Finding and facing the cause or causes of your physical problem paves the way for divine healing. Even so the cause should not be your primary focus. Be encouraged that the risen Lord Jesus Christ knows how to diagnose your case. He knows how to probe your wound. He is well able to discern the cause of your trouble and expose the source. As the Great Physician, He can also apply the right remedy in the right proportion. *Let Christ the Healer be the center of your attention.*

Reflections

1. What is the cause of your physical malady?
2. What specific direction in prayer might this suggest?
3. Is your primary focus on Christ the Healer?

Prayer

God, I am trying to discern any underlying root cause for my physical illness—spiritual or physical, mental or emotional, hurts or habits, personal or family sins, divine discipline or demonic activity, accident or defect, neglect or abuse, improper diet or inadequate exercise or old age. Search me, O God. *Deal gently with me—with anything that may not be right before You. I know that the risen Christ knows how to diagnose my case, probe my wound, discern the cause of my trouble, expose the source and then apply the right remedy in the right proportion. Hallelujah! Christ is the Healer of my body!*

8

Barriers

Are You Removing Barriers to Healing?

A Sunday school teacher had just reviewed the day's lesson. "And now, children, who can tell me what we must do before we can expect forgiveness of sin?" There was a pause, but finally one little boy spoke up: "Well, first we've got to sin."

After you have discerned the cause of your sickness, which provides direction for prayer, you must remove any barriers to healing. These barriers often involve sin and they can prevent God's divine intervention. A list of potential barriers could be endless. We will discuss twelve that are the most common.

Twelve Barriers to Healing

If you are serious about asking the Holy Spirit to show you any pattern of wrong living or sin in your life, He will do so. The following is a list of twelve barriers and the actions to take concerning them. Would you review this list slowly and prayerfully in the presence of God? Ask God to search your heart. See if there is any offensive way in you. Then begin taking the appropriate action.

- *Is there sin in your life that you have kept hidden?*
  Repent of harbored and unconfessed sin.
- *Have you refused to forgive someone?*
  Forgive those who have offended you.
- *Do you harbor a "bad attitude" about a person or situation?*
  Remove false or wrongful attitudes.
- *Are you using the wrong motivation in your pursuit of a desire or dream?*
  Abandon impure motives.
- *Do you owe someone something? An apology? A financial reimbursement?*
  Make restitution toward others.
- *Are you letting stress or fear determine what decisions you make?*
  Learn how to handle negative emotional or psychological responses to pressure.
- *Do you accept attacks by the enemy as inevitable?*
  Rebuke demonic attacks.
- *Have you ever participated in any occult activity?*
  Renounce occult participation or practices.
- *Do you allow ungodly thought patterns to play in your mind?*
  Replace ungodly thought patterns.
- *Do you continue in a behavior that you know—or suspect—is counter to God's will?*
  Change lifestyles or habits that displease God.
- *Have you refused or neglected to obey a direct word from God?*
  Obey the specific commands God has given you.
- *Do you resist the disciplinary work of the Holy Spirit?*
  Respond to the corrective measures brought into your life by the Holy Spirit.

It is possible to have more than one issue to deal with in each of the twelve categories. You may, for instance, have more than one unconfessed sin or more than one habit that displeases God. Deal with them all. Remove every spiritual or psychological block to healing. The Bible does not link all sickness to any particular sin, but sometimes sin or patterns of wrong living can produce hindrances that need to be removed.

Your Attitude Can Help

In a survey of hostile communities, the Gallup Organization concluded that anger can be hazardous to your health. In this study, Philadelphia ranked first among U.S. cities on what they called the "hostility index." Based on a nine-question scale, they asked people how they felt about such things as loud rock music, supermarket checkout lines and traffic jams. The next four cities on the hostility list were New York, Cleveland, Chicago and Detroit. At the bottom of the hostility index were Des Moines, Minneapolis, Denver, Seattle and Honolulu. (For those of you who live in one of these cities, aren't you glad!)

Looking at the results, medical experts found it no coincidence that the cities high on the hostility index also had higher death rates. Commenting on the study, Dr. Redford Williams of Duke University Medical School said: "Anger kills. There is a strong correlation between hostility and death rates. The angrier people are and the more cynical they are, the shorter their life span."[1]

Further evidence within the healthcare profession indicates that beliefs and feelings have powerful effects on the body, especially on the immune system. Unresolved guilt, anger, resentment and meaninglessness suppress your immune system, while loving relationships within community build it up.

Since human beings are wired for God, a healthy Christian spirituality often produces physical benefits. Belief can create a positive emotional state that reverses harmful mental or physical conditions and promotes health. Statistically, people who hold to a particular faith and attend religious services have generally better health than those who do not.

In 1997 an American Heart Association journal reported significant findings in this area. Susan Everson, research scientist at the Human Population Laboratory of the Public Health Institute in Berkeley, California, learned that middle-aged men who experienced high levels of despair had a twenty percent greater occurrence of narrowed arteries than did optimistic men. Everson said, "This is the same magnitude of increased risk that one sees in comparing a pack-a-day smoker to a nonsmoker."[2] In other words, despair can be as bad for you as smoking a pack of cigarettes a day! Yes, a Christian attitude of hope contributes to good health.

Emotional or psychological responses to pressure that are self-destructive—such as depression, fear, hopelessness, self-pity—need to be redirected because they quench faith. Strained relationships need to be reconciled, for it is within community that God heals you. When you are weak physically, you are more likely to be weakened emotionally and vulnerable spiritually. Your overall condition of suffering can make you susceptible to demonic attacks from which you need to find release. Do you see what I mean by barriers?

Ronald Reagan's forgiving attitude after the 1982 attempt on his life made an impression on his daughter Patti Davis:

The following day . . . my father said . . . he knew his physical healing was directly dependent on his ability to forgive John Hinckley. . . . By showing me that forgiveness is the key to everything, including physical health and healing, he gave me an example of Christ-like thinking. Forgiving is the antidote for anger, fear, and every form of hatred. I think of it as a force so huge, so powerful, that it can only lead to miracles.[3]

Review again that list of actions to take concerning the twelve possible barriers and see which ones, if any, stand out. Don't be among those who resist confronting an issue that is a barrier to healing.

Get Right with God and with Others

Your goal at this point in your journey toward healing is to get right with God and with others. Make amends. Decide that you will live the way God wants you to live from this day forward. Don't put it off. Do it now.

People under pressure can come up with some very creative excuses! Here is a list of statements made by motorists who were trying to explain why they had been involved in accidents:

- "The other car collided with mine without giving warning of its intentions."
- "A pedestrian hit me and went under my car."
- "Coming home I drove into the wrong house and collided with a tree I don't have."
- "I pulled away from the side of the road, glanced at my mother-in-law and headed over the embankment."
- "The pedestrian had no idea which direction to run, so I ran over him."
- "The indirect cause of the accident was a little guy in a small car with a big mouth."

80

These humorous excuses show how prone we are to evade responsibility for our wrong actions. They are typical attempts to justify a mistake and escape blame.

I know that some Christians have overactive consciences. Taking a hard look at their hearts is difficult for them because they end up overwhelmed by their faults. While the Lord does not demand perfection, He does expect us to be sincere in our desire to please Him. God does expect us to walk in the light He has given us.

Obey the Lord humbly. Obey His will to the best knowledge you have of His Word. Obey Him in specific areas that His Spirit applies to you. Live from now on in the light God gives you.

Perhaps you need to die to your own selfishness and pride, forgive someone who offended you, reorder your priorities, cast out fears, overcome doubt and unbelief, or get rid of worry, anger, bitterness, hatred or resentment.

Get right with God and with others. This is a condition for healing. Furthermore, you can only safely keep your healing as you keep your heart and life holy before God.

Press beyond the Barriers

Some people in the gospels used aggressive means to get to Jesus for healing. Luke describes such an occasion when the power of the Lord was present for Jesus to heal the sick (see 5:17). Four men had a friend who was paralyzed. To get their friend to Jesus, they literally broke through the roof of a house.

Some men came carrying a paralytic on a mat and tried to take him into the house to lay him before Jesus. When

81

they could not find a way to do this because of the crowd, they went up on the roof and lowered him on his mat through the tiles into the middle of the crowd, right in front of Jesus. When Jesus saw their faith, he said, "Friend, your sins are forgiven."

Luke 5:18–20

Notice that Jesus saw *their* faith, the faith of the paralytic man *and* his friends, and He responded by healing the paralytic. Jesus was healing others, and this man and his friends dared not lose the opportunity. But physical and spiritual barriers had to be removed. This paralyzed man needed to be brought to Jesus. He also needed to get right with God. After forgiving the man's sins, Jesus healed him.

Get aggressive about seeking the Lord to heal you. Press beyond the barriers. Like these four men, break through the ceiling of obstructions until you can reach the Person of Christ. Like the woman who pressed through the crowd until she touched the hem of Jesus' garment, elbow your way through the crowd until you come directly to Christ the Healer.

Press beyond sin and selfishness and satanic attacks. Press beyond lukewarmness and disobedience and unconfessed sins. Press beyond repeated stumbling stones and habitual sins. Press beyond the opinion of others against divine healing and those who are afraid of it. Press beyond personal doubts and fears. Press beyond symptoms and feelings and lying evil spirits.

Remember, Jesus is the Healer and you want the Lord to heal you. Deal ruthlessly with any and all barriers and obstacles and sins. Press through these things as if you are striding through a cloud of gnats. Only get through. Don't let some little sin keep you from a big blessing. Press toward a faith that wants only what God wants for you. Press forward until you touch God!

Reflections

1. What barrier do you need to remove? Where do you need to get right with God or with others? Has the Lord mentioned one sin here? Have you confessed and forsaken it?
2. What specific actions do you need to take?
3. How can you press beyond the barriers?

Prayer

God, I desire to remove any and all barriers, obstacles or sins that may interfere with or prevent Your divine touch in my body. Holy Spirit, I open myself to Your examination, Your conviction, Your prompting. I want to respond humbly and obediently to whatever You want to say to me. I promise to live the way You want me to live from this day forward. I choose to use this sickness as an opportunity to get right with You and to live from now on in the light You give me. Pressing my way forward, I come to Christ the Healer.

9
Deliberation

Have You Thoroughly Prepared Your Inner Life?

As you seek the Lord for healing, you are moving toward a particular culminating moment. It is not unlike a marriage ceremony. Before the healing event when others pray for you, you are taking every step carefully and weighing every aspect thoroughly before God.

I encourage you to review in your mind all the issues you have already processed: biblical concepts you have thought through; spiritual decisions you have made; holy desires you have nurtured. You are making an interior review of all that God has been doing in you related to your physical condition. You may want to write these things down. If you are worried that you will leave out something important, don't be. The Holy Spirit will show you. After this process you should consider all these questions between you and God forever settled.

Deliberate preparation of the inner life for physical healing breeds both quietness and praise. As you consider the seriousness of your request, you will feel an inward sense of *quietness*. As you look forward to what God may do, you will also feel a growing sense of *praise*.

Interior Rest

As you reflect on all that has transpired, you may discover that your soul is moving into a state of *stasis*. A spiritual stasis is a state of quiet waiting before God. You have now dealt with and set behind you all necessary issues, concerns and sins. You know inwardly that the preparation stage is ending. You wonder how that seed of faith is ripening within you. It is ready to blossom. The winter of your soul is ending. Spring is coming. You now only have to commit your whole person to God and ask.

Listen to the Bible writers describe this quieting of the soul before God.

He makes me lie down in green pastures, he leads me beside quiet waters.

Psalm 23:2

"Be still, and know that I am God."

Psalm 46:10

I wait for the LORD, my soul waits, and in his word I put my hope. My soul waits for the LORD more than watchmen wait for the morning, more than watchmen wait for the morning.

Psalm 130:5–6

But I have stilled and quieted my soul; like a weaned child with its mother, like a weaned child is my soul within me.

Psalm 131:2

85

This is what the Sovereign LORD, the Holy One of Israel, says: "In repentance and rest is your salvation, in quietness and trust is your strength."

Isaiah 30:15

It is good to wait quietly for the salvation of the LORD.

Lamentations 3:26

"The LORD your God is with you, he is mighty to save. He will take great delight in you, he will quiet you with his love, he will rejoice over you with singing."

Zephaniah 3:17

"Come to me, all you who are weary and burdened, and I will give you rest. Take my yoke upon you and learn from me, for I am gentle and humble in heart, and you will find rest for your souls. For my yoke is easy and my burden is light."

Matthew 11:28–30

As you read and reflect on these verses, can you feel your inner being slowing down, getting quiet, coming into the posture of rest before the Lord? Everything you have processed before the Lord is culminating in quiet waiting. You sense that you are moving to an end of this preparation phase and that the Lord is readying you for the next phase of encounter. In that quietness, silence and stillness, you wait before the Lord. A nineteenth-century hymn celebrates this dynamic of spirituality:

> Blessed quietness, holy quietness,
> What assurance in my soul!
> On the stormy sea He speaks peace to me,
> How the billows [waves] cease to roll![1]

As you are seeking the Lord for healing, you discover an inner quiet beneath the turbulence, a constant during the flux, a stillness during great activity. In a word, you have *peace*. You are experiencing in part what Paul described in Philippians 4:7, when he referred to "the peace of God, which transcends all understanding, [that] will guard your hearts and your minds in Christ Jesus." John Greenleaf Whittier understood this as he prayed:

> Drop Thy still dews of quietness,
> Till all our strivings cease;
> Take from our souls the strain and stress,
> And let our ordered lives confess
> The beauty of Thy peace.[2]

This interior quieting of the soul does not guarantee how or when or if God will heal you. God's perfect will for your life might not include healing. You cannot manipulate, trick, force or command God to act for you. Yet you know you are coming to a position of rest whatever God does or does not do. The posture of your soul is one of waiting in expectation before the Lord. Your eyes are upon God alone. Don't think of this stage, this resignation to the Lord's perfect will, as the death of healing. It is, rather, the stage right before the birth of healing.

Upward Praise

James H. Brookes said, "Sickness is a rough but thorough teacher of experimental theology, and it almost compels the soul of the believer to stay itself upon God." Shortly before Scottish missionary John G. Paton died, a friend said to him, "I am sorry to see you lying on your back." Smiling, Paton asked, "Do you know why God puts us on our backs?" After his friend answered no, the missionary replied, "In order that we may look upward!"

In the mystery of healing, an almost paradoxical interior movement is taking place. Your quiet heart suddenly comes to a turning point and breaks out in verbal praise. Perhaps while you are worshiping the Lord at home or in a church service, your faith quickens. God fills your mouth with praise, not for what He *has* done and *is* doing, but for who He is and what He *may* do.

I cannot explain how it works. It is as if the wellspring of your soul has been silently flowing downstream and all of a sudden it thunders with the power of a waterfall. Your prayerful desires go down, down, deeper and deeper into your own soul and deeper and deeper into God and then suddenly turn a corner and explode into praise.

Previous negative thought patterns dissolve. Ways of thinking biblically develop. A spirit of praise is not a tool to manipulate God to act for you. Through praise you attune yourself to the harmony of His plan.

The quietness comes because you have settled things with God. As you become aware of the Lord's presence, this new praise comes as His gift. If this has not yet come, don't worry. As you quiet yourself in the presence of God, a spirit of praise will come. It is the birth of expectation.

A Musical Miracle

Filipino pastor Oscar Montillana and his coworkers were awed by the beauty of God's creation as they crossed a scenic lake on their way to conduct evangelism. As their boat slowly sliced through the water, they were moved to worship the Lord for His delicate handiwork. One began playing the guitar and another played the tambourine. They sang out praises to God.

Not far from them a large fishing boat was anchored. On it sat a lonely, hurting man. He suffered terribly from back pain. As the sounds of the sweet music floated across the waters, he lifted his eyes and tuned his ears. The melodies uplifted him and helped him escape the agony he had endured so long. As he became engrossed in the heavenly music, his pain drifted away. Suddenly he realized that the pain had disappeared. In astonishment he quickly maneuvered his boat toward these unknown singers. With gratitude he offered them some fish, blurting out the miracle that had just occurred.

Oscar said, "We shared with him the Word of God and told him about the greatness of the Lord." With newfound faith and joy the man said, "Jesus is not only the Savior, but also the Healer."[3]

Your own song of exultation breathes a spirit of expectation. Your grateful heart prepares you to receive from the Lord. You anticipate that God's presence and power will energize the prayer of faith by other believers. Your expectation in God to heal you is ripening and nearly ready to yield its fruit.

Reflections

1. Are there any steps you have left out? Ask God.
2. Describe your inner world of quiet waiting before the Lord.
3. Has your soul shifted yet into praise? Describe this new dimension.

Prayer

God, I want deliberately to prepare my inner life to receive physical healing—to weigh all issues thoroughly, to set them all behind me and to regard them as forever settled. I feel a sense of quietness. *I review in my mind how I have come to this point. I do not want to leave out any steps. My soul waits in silence before You. I wonder at that seed of faith beginning to ripen and becoming ready to blossom within me. I also feel a sense of* praise, *not for what You* have *done and* are *doing, but for what You* may *do. I find my heart tuning itself to the harmony of Your plan with a spirit of expectation. My heart is beginning to overflow with gratefulness. My mouth is beginning to sing and shout praises to You, the Lord most High!*

10
Commitment

Are You Ready to Give Yourself Totally to God?

Need. Want. Lessons. Scripture. Love. Faith. Cause. Barriers. Deliberation.

Are you feeling that the journey toward physical healing is too long and involved? You may be saying to yourself, *I'm finally at step number ten, and I haven't yet involved the prayers of others!*

Let me encourage you to *press on.* You will not regret the thoroughness of your personal preparation. In reality there are not always multiple steps to healing. In your case, there may be only one or perhaps two primary areas that the Lord wants you to face. The gospels record the healings of Jesus to show us that in different situations the Lord needed to emphasize different things for different people. For one it was clarifying the person's desire. For another it was being assured of God's love. For yet another it was confronting a sin issue, and so on. In one sense, all these fall under the umbrella of faith.

Be assured that *because* God has been working with you, you can be confident that God will meet your specific need.

When Francis of Assisi (1182–1226), founder of the Franciscan Order, came to the town of Toscanella on the road to Rome, a knight gave him hospitality. This knight had a crippled son who was suffering throughout his entire body. Moved by the urgency of the knight's appeals, Francis laid his hands on the boy and blessed him. At the same moment the boy "stood upright and firm on his legs, and was entirely cured, to the great astonishment of his whole family."[1]

God Is Leading You

I have long been fascinated by the story of the man born blind whom Jesus healed. John 9 describes his journey toward faith, or perhaps the journey on which God was taking him. *It encourages me to see God leading you and drawing you to the place He desires.* Notice this blind man's growing understanding in the four statements he made about Jesus, in italics below, after he was healed.

He replied, *"The man they call Jesus* made some mud and put it on my eyes. He told me to go to Siloam and wash. So I went and washed, and then I could see" (John 9:11).	At first he was uncertain of Jesus' true identity. He acknowledged that others called Him Jesus.
Finally they turned again to the blind man, "What have you to say about him? It was your eyes he opened." The man replied, *"He is a prophet"* (John 9:17).	Next he concluded that Jesus must be a prophet, perhaps the highest designation he could think of.
"Nobody has ever heard of opening the eyes of a man born blind. If this man were not *from God,* he could do nothing" (John 9:32–33).	He further realized that only if this man, this prophet, was from God could He open blind eyes. He reasoned that this one must have been sent from God.
Then the man said, *"Lord, I believe,"* and he worshiped him (John 9:38).	Finally, he worshiped Jesus as Lord, as the Son of Man and the Son of God. He believed.

Did you notice his faith development in understanding Jesus? From man to prophet to one sent from God to Lord. Likewise, God is the one who is leading you on a journey toward the goal He has in mind. You may only see it all as you look back. For the moment, like the Thomas A. Dorsey song, let the Lord take your hand as He leads you.

> Precious Lord, take my hand,
> Lead me on, help me stand—
> I am tired, I am weak, I am worn;
> Thro' the storm, thro' the night,
> Lead me on to the light—
> Take my hand, precious Lord, lead me home.

You may feel physically weary and emotionally exhausted. Let me encourage you to press on. You are almost there. While the Lord is leading you homeward to the purpose He has designed, you have one last preparation step to take.

Commit Your Whole Person to God

The last factor in the preparation phase is a full, final and definitive commitment of your whole self to God. All your heart preparation now culminates here. By a conscious act of your will, you present your whole person, and specifically your body, to God. Paul wrote:

> Therefore, I urge you, brothers, in view of God's mercy, to offer your bodies as living sacrifices, holy and pleasing to God—this is your spiritual act of worship.
>
> Romans 12:1

You want God to own your total being. You affirm that your body is no longer yours but God's. You give up all rights of ownership. You give every cell, nerve, tissue,

93

muscle, bone and organ over to God. You dedicate your body, a temple of the Holy Spirit, to the Lord.

You might ask: "I've already given myself over to God. I totally surrendered myself to God at a church service. Why do I need to do this again?" Because this special consecration of your body to God is separate from other commitments you have made to Him. It has a specific purpose.

God Fills What You Give

Paul's words in 1 Corinthians 6:13, "The body is . . . for the Lord," mean that you are giving yourself one hundred percent to God as a living sacrifice. His further expression in that verse, "The Lord [is] for the body," means that God accepts your offering and by the Holy Spirit the Lord Jesus will impart strength to your body. As you surrender, God fills.

You see, healing and the work of the Holy Spirit are closely intertwined. When you give yourself to God, God fills you with His Holy Spirit. As you receive His presence and power into your inner life, His life and power will also overflow into your physical being. God's living presence will touch every part of you—spirit, soul and body. Every fiber of your body may feel the life of the risen Lord Jesus flowing in.

Handing over your body to God in full surrender and perfect trust is an exchange of your weakness for His strength! It is an exchange of your disability for His ability! It is an exchange of your diseased life for an impartation of the resurrected life of Jesus!

Closing Thoughts about Preparation

Let me give you some closing thoughts about all these preparatory steps. Some people are not ready to be healed. Others have to deal with personal baggage. Still others need to nurture faith.

This preparation phase of heart and mind may take a week, a month or only a brief moment. Often the more serious your physical condition or the longer you have carried an illness, the greater the time of preparation.

Sometimes God heals people *without* processing any of these outlined "steps." And sometimes God does *not* heal people in spite of their diligence to work their way through them all. Their healing will come at the resurrection when their bodies will be redeemed (see Romans 8:23).

In the book *His Mysterious Ways*, Margaret Murray tells this story about her uncle. In September, Uncle Wilson, her mother's only brother, underwent surgery for an intestinal tumor. The doctors, discovering that the tumor was too large and complex to remove, gave him from four to six months to live. Uncle Wilson was brought home to spend his remaining days. With no wife to see to his needs, his care fell to Margaret, her mother, her two sisters and the nieces and nephews.

They all worked hard to make Uncle Wilson comfortable, but he was bedridden, helpless and in great pain. Day after day they tended to his needs and tried to soothe his fears. Every night before bed, Margaret knelt and asked God to heal this good, kind man.

In July, ten hard months having passed, Uncle Wilson took a turn for the worse. Margaret was told to come at once. She stood by his bed, waiting for the ambulance. Even in his pain Uncle Wilson tried to communicate his love and thanks by kissing her hand.

By now Margaret was no longer praying for his healing but simply asking that God take her uncle to be with Him in heaven. And then, early in the morning of his third day in the hospital, she and her sister were with Uncle Wilson when suddenly he opened his eyes, and in a loud, clear voice cried, "My God! My God! My God!" They were "wonderstruck."

Uncle Wilson died soon after, but the family members were awed by the sense that they had had a preview of the healing that awaited him. You see, Uncle Wilson had been deaf and mute since birth. Those words were the first he had ever spoken.[2]

Some healings will not take place in this lifetime. Even as our ability to reason does not guarantee our ability to understand, personal preparation does not guarantee healing. Even the "best" preparation may lead to greater spiritual vitality without physical healing. God's ways are beyond our ways. Healing and faith are still mysteries.

Sometimes good and godly Christians get sick, suffer and die. And sometimes unprincipled and unbelieving people get better, stay well, live long and prosper.

Taking all these steps does not measure how great your faith is. Nor does healing prove how spiritual you are. The greatness of your faith or the goodness of your virtues does not command God's response, for we are *His* servants. "For it is *God* who works in you to will and to act according to his good purpose" (Philippians 2:13, emphasis added).

Still, all that said, I believe the Lord wants to heal many more people than are healed. Jesus looks for faith: "When the Son of Man comes, will he find faith on the earth?" (Luke 18:8).

Preparing your heart and mind gives the Lord more freedom to work in you. It is like clearing the runway so the plane can land. How often I have wished that people would prepare themselves more thoroughly for divine healing! The preparation phase leads to the healing event. This I can guarantee: Whatever happens, you will have a deep and lasting encounter with the Lord Jesus Christ.

Miracles Do Happen

In 1993 the late author and church leader John Wimber found he had inoperable cancer and underwent radiation treatments. The cancer went into remission. In *Living with Uncertainty* he wrote about not receiving a miraculous healing for himself even though he had seen others dramatically healed by God.

Wimber was speaking in South Africa at a large conference. A friend, John McClure, was with him, and they were asked to visit a woman who was a church member there. She was dressed beautifully but was emaciated and weighed only about 85 pounds. The hospital had sent her home to die. Her body was full of cancer. Her only hope of survival was divine intervention.

They prayed for her, not with great fervency, but they did pray. John McClure had confidence that she would be healed, but Wimber felt nothing.

That night she woke up with a vibrant, tingling feeling throughout her entire body. For the next four hours her body was full of intense heat. She tried to call out to her husband in the next room, but she could not raise her voice loud enough for him to hear.

Alone and frightened, she crawled into the bathroom, her body racked with pain. At the time she thought, *O my God. My body is coming apart and I'm dying.* In reality, she was eliminating from her body a number of large tumors. Finally, exhausted from the events of that night, she fell back asleep. She did not know if she would wake up.

But half an hour later she woke up incredibly refreshed. Later her husband woke to the smell of brewing coffee. He asked, "What are you doing?" He was astonished to see his wife on her feet and preparing breakfast.

She replied with sudden understanding: "God has healed me."

Two days later she reported to her doctors, who gave her a clean bill of health. They could not find any cancer in her body. God had completely delivered her from it all.

Without much energy to pray on their part and without great faith on her part, the Lord chose to heal this woman's cancer-infested body supernaturally.[3]

Miracles do happen.

Reflections

1. Can you trace the path on which God has led you so far?
2. Are you ready to give yourself totally to God?
3. What image do you see in the infilling of the Holy Spirit?

Prayer

God, I now make a full, final and definitive commitment of my total person, and specifically my body, to You. I belong to You. Every part of my body I give to You in full surrender and perfect trust. I dedicate this temple for Your pleasure and glory. My body is for You, Lord— *wholly given over and offered in sacrifice to You.* You, Lord, are for my body—*I know that as You accept my offering by Your Spirit You will impart Your own strength to my body. I surrender myself to You for a fresh infilling of Your Holy Spirit that will overflow into every part of my physical body until every cell feels the touch of Your life and power. I am ready to exchange my weakness for Your strength and my disability for Your ability, and to receive the resurrected life of Jesus.*

During Prayer for Healing

After working your way up through the forest of personal preparation, your journey is taking you higher and nearer to the summit: the healing event. The cultivation of your faith now begins to bear fruit. You will have a personal encounter with the risen and ascended Lord Jesus Christ.

You have been responsible for doing all that can be done to prepare the way for God to do what only God can do. Like John the Baptist you have prepared the way for the Lord to come and work in power.

A lot is happening all at once in this phase—specific faith, prayer by others, precise asking, authoritative faith, triggers of faith, encountering the risen Christ.

You are not alone. Trusted believers will gather around you. The Christian community will stand with you. The Lord Jesus Himself will come to you.

There is hope for a cure. Your faith may be the very spark that ignites the fire of God to fall upon you.

11

Readiness

*Which Scriptures Are You Claiming
for Your Healing?*

John Wesley (1703–1791), founder of Methodism, recorded his personal experience with healing: "On
twenty-four occasions the Lord's hand healed my
bodily illnesses, which enabled me to continue travel-
ing and preaching."[1] Wesley exercised his faith to receive
healing numerous times!

Healing faith is different from saving faith. Saving
faith is exercised once as you call on the Lord to be
saved. Healing faith is a specific faith nurtured for a
specific situation. This specific faith is an expression
of your readiness to receive from the Lord.

Where does this faith come from? Similar to salvation,
this faith comes from the Word of God. "Consequently,
faith comes from hearing the message, and the message
is heard through the word of Christ" (Romans 10:17).
Faith for healing often comes from a specific Bible text
or Bible character. As you read and reflect on various
Bible passages, you may find yourself gravitating toward
one in particular. A promise from the Bible may seem
specifically illuminated. You may personally identify
with a particular Bible person.

People seeking the Lord for healing are frequently drawn to the gospel stories of Jesus' healings, stories, for example, like the one of the woman with a hemorrhage who wants to touch the hem of Jesus' garment:

> So Jesus went with him. A large crowd followed and pressed around him. And a woman was there who had been subject to bleeding for twelve years. She had suffered a great deal under the care of many doctors and had spent all she had, yet instead of getting better she grew worse. When she heard about Jesus, she came up behind him in the crowd and touched his cloak, because she thought, "If I just touch his clothes, I will be healed." Immediately her bleeding stopped and she felt in her body that she was freed from her suffering. At once Jesus realized that power had gone out from him. He turned around in the crowd and asked, "Who touched my clothes?" "You see the people crowding against you," his disciples answered, "and yet you can ask, 'Who touched me?'" But Jesus kept looking around to see who had done it. Then the woman, knowing what had happened to her, came and fell at his feet and, trembling with fear, told him the whole truth. He said to her, "Daughter, your faith has healed you. Go in peace and be freed from your suffering."
>
> Mark 5:24–34

Perhaps the notion of reaching out to touch Jesus as He passes by has gripped you. Or perhaps you are drawn to the story of blind Bartimaeus who wants to receive his sight. You are especially captivated by Jesus' question, "What do you want Me to do for you?" You identify strongly with Bartimaeus' persistence, which climaxes with his specific request:

> Then they came to Jericho. As Jesus and his disciples, together with a large crowd, were leaving the city, a blind man, Bartimaeus (that is, the Son of Timaeus),

was sitting by the roadside begging. When he heard that it was Jesus of Nazareth, he began to shout, "Jesus, Son of David, have mercy on me!" Many rebuked him and told him to be quiet, but he shouted all the more, "Son of David, have mercy on me!" Jesus stopped and said, "Call him." So they called to the blind man, "Cheer up! On your feet! He's calling you." Throwing his cloak aside, he jumped to his feet and came to Jesus. "What do you want me to do for you?" Jesus asked him. The blind man said, "Rabbi, I want to see." "Go," said Jesus, "your faith has healed you." Immediately he received his sight and followed Jesus along the road.

Mark 10:46–52

Spend time reviewing the gospel stories of Jesus' healing ministry. You can find that list in Appendix 1: The Healing Ministry of Jesus Christ in the Gospels. My point is this: After grasping the general biblical truth about healing, you lay hold of some specific Bible passage or verse. You identify with *that* person or you apply *that* verse to yourself by faith. It must be specific. You soak yourself in the Word and listen to the Spirit until you receive a word from the Lord. The psalmist declared, "He sent forth his *word* and healed them" (Psalm 107:20, emphasis added).

Famous English evangelist George Whitefield (1714–1770) wrote in his journal: "I began to read the Holy Scriptures upon my knees, laying aside all other books, and praying over, if possible, every line and word. This proved meat indeed, and drink indeed, to my soul. I daily received fresh life, light and power from above."[2]

As you read and reflect on Bible passages about healing, imagine one hundred ropes hanging from heaven. You cannot grab them all, nor do you need to. But you can take hold of one. Grip that one firmly until it brings you heaven's blessing.

A Divine Mystery

You may wonder how this works. So do I. *Connecting with the divine in healing is a mystery.* In spite of the power of scientific investigation, science will never erase all the mystery that surrounds healing. Some have wondered if we can measure the power of prayer, or if we can bring God into the laboratory for analysis. That is what Dr. Randolph Byrd, cardiologist and faculty member of the University of California Medical School, set out to demonstrate in his 1994 landmark study of four hundred heart-attack patients. The patients were divided into two groups, both receiving state-of-the-art medical treatment. But one group was prayed for by various prayer groups and the other was not. Neither nurses, physicians nor patients knew who was and was not being prayed for.

The patients who were prayed for showed marked improvement in several areas. They were less likely to develop congestive heart failure or to require antibiotics or breathing tubes. Fewer of these patients developed pneumonia or experienced cardiac arrest than those who were not prayed for. Still, scientific studies of prayer and illness aside, science will never erase all the paradoxes and mysteries surrounding healing.[3]

Let me state it again: *Connecting with the divine in healing is a mystery.* Within Christian spirituality, somehow through the Word of God and by the Spirit of God, you find yourself in the arena of faith. When the Lord has led you to a particular Scripture passage or biblical person, the divine Healer appears for *you*. You unite with that ancient community of the saints. You identify with their experiences. Their encounters with the living God uniquely become your personal experience.

As you see yourself in a similar situation, you expect God to do the same thing for you. Jesus healed the sick and cured the lame. You anticipate the same kind of healing happening to you. As you reach out in faith to God, God reaches down in love to you. God comes to you *in* your experience. Building upon historic faith and objective truth, your personal faith is realized. Biblical doctrine evokes Christian experience.

Ask God for Specific Faith

If your faith is weak, *ask God* to give you specific faith for healing. Healing is a distinctive gift from God. Faith for healing is not a purely human act, nor is it the product of inner willpower. You cannot make yourself believe, nor can you force faith. That would be faith in faith, not faith in God. You cannot insist on healing because healing is always a gift from God. Only God knows all the factors in heaven and on earth, past, present and future, why healing should or should not take place.

True faith is founded on the Word of God and is made alive to you by the Spirit of God. Because you have been diligent in preparing your inner life, cultivating the soil of your heart, you are a prime candidate for a divine touch. Now ask God for specific faith for your healing.

Besides, it is not *much faith* God requires, but *real faith*. Jesus said, "If you have faith as small as a mustard seed, you can say to this mulberry tree, 'Be uprooted and planted in the sea,' and it will obey you" (Luke 17:6). Jesus emphasized the *quality* of faith, not its size. A faith full of trust, believing without doubting, is the kind of faith God is seeking to find in you. Practically speaking, that expression of faith may sometimes emerge from you and sometimes from others as they pray for you.

What Faith for Healing Is Not

Clarifying what faith for healing is *not* is important. Some have wrongly promoted the idea that it is the will of God to heal all who believe. They say that God's highest will is always to heal. *But a promise from the Bible is not necessarily God's direct message to you, unless God's Spirit has clearly applied it to you!* Nor will you automatically possess everything you confess. Constantly repeating a Bible verse like a mantra is not some magical formula for healing. Even following a series of biblical steps does not guarantee healing.

In addition, healing does not mean that you will live in perfect health. Healing is not a fountain of youth. If Jesus heals you at eighty, you will not feel as though you are eighteen. Of all the miracles Jesus did, He never made an older person into a younger person. The aging process and death are realities. Faith for healing is neither stupid nor presumptuous.

Invisible Healing

Even honest faith, strong or weak, does not always result in *visible* healing. Sometimes there is no lack of faith in the seeker or the pray-ers. But the individual does not get any better and may even get worse and die. The faith solution in these cases may ultimately be found in the innocent suffering of Job:

> "Naked I came from my mother's womb, and naked I will depart. The LORD gave and the LORD has taken away; may the name of the LORD be praised." In all this, Job did not sin by charging God with wrongdoing.
>
> Job 1:21–22

In these cases some *invisible* healing often takes place in response to faith. The inner life or the human psyche may receive a genuine and even profound touch from the risen Jesus.

106

Discerning God's Will for You

Considering the context of the whole Bible, you need to discern prayerfully the will and mind of God for your healing. This will also be the goal of those praying for you. You cannot take healing for granted. Ask God what He intends to do for you and then listen for His answer.

Like the prophet Habakkuk, ask God and then "look to see what he will say to" you (2:1). Wait in the presence of God until you have a word from Him. Linger in His presence until the Holy Spirit speaks to you. Seek God's face until He tells you what He wants to say to you.

This word that comes through the Word of God by the Spirit of God will be your answer as to whether God will heal you or not. It is true—sometimes God says *no*. Sometimes He says: "*No*, I love you too much. I have a different plan." But sometimes God says: "No, not yet. *Wait* a while. Keep asking."

God always answers our prayers. Our prayers always bring results. Even the "no" and the "wait" can be demonstrations of God's purposes and power.

But how often we miss the biggest blessings of all when God is shouting, "*Yes*, and I thought you would never ask!" Or better yet, God says, "*Yes*, and here's more!" When Jesus speaks that word, you can be assured, He will heal you!

God will either give you divine *healing that quickens* your body or give you divine *grace that enables you to live above* your affliction. Either way you win. This is Romans 8:11 in action: "And if the Spirit of him who raised Jesus from the dead is living in you, he who raised Christ from the dead will also give life to your mortal bodies through his Spirit, who lives in you." *Seek to be healed until God either heals you or tells you why not.*

Healing and Grace Given

David Livingstone (1813–1873), one of the greatest missionaries and explorers in modern times, opened half of Africa to Christianity. After the University of Glasgow conferred the degree of Doctor of Laws on Livingstone, he addressed a gathering of students. He bore on his body the marks of his African struggles. Severe illness on nearly thirty occasions had left him gaunt and haggard. His left arm, which a lion had crushed, hung limp at his side.

After describing his trials and tribulations, Livingstone said: "Would you like me to tell you what supported me through all the years of exile among people whose language I could not understand, and whose attitude towards me was always uncertain and often hostile? It was this: 'Lo, I am with you alway, even unto the end of the world.' On these words I staked everything, and they never failed!"[4]

God's Word never fails. Seek specific faith for your specific situation. Rooting your faith within a specific Scripture text that the Spirit of God has uniquely applied to you, or identifying with a Bible person whom God has healed, will serve as a springboard to the apex you desire to reach. Be convinced in your heart that God wants to heal you unless He has shown you otherwise. Be clear about God's specific will for you in your particular sickness. Then get ready. Be assured. When others pray in faith for you, the Lord will raise you up.

Reflections

1. Which Bible passage have you applied to your situation or which Bible person have you identified with?

2. Are you asking God for specific faith for your healing?
3. What is God saying specifically to you?

Prayer

God, I am waiting in Your presence for a definite word from Christ for my specific situation now. I want to discern Your perfect will for me in this circumstance. Grant to me specific faith. I am listening to You for an answer—to claim a specific Bible promise or identify with an applicable Bible person. I know I cannot make myself believe, force faith or insist on healing, for healing is a distinctive gift from You. I will either seek to be healed until I am healed or be confident You will give me an answer why I am not healed. What do You intend to do? *In any case, I am assured that I will receive a genuine touch from Jesus. Either way I win.*

Others

Have You Called Others to Pray?

After nurturing specific faith for your healing, you are now primed to call upon others from your church to pray for you.

Now, let me mention here that if you suddenly face a severe headache at work or find yourself fighting a cold at school or have stomach pains at home, the first thing to do is to pray *yourself*! Before describing the healing ministry of the Church, James first says, "Is any one of you in trouble [or afflicted]? He should pray" (5:13).

We are often quick to activate the church prayer chain or ask someone to pray concerning our physical needs— and this is a normal response because God answers the prayers of the saints! But we should never neglect to pray for our own physical needs. We miss opportunities to bring God into the small stuff of life.

When more aggressive prayer for more pronounced needs is in order, however, it is time to take the next step.

Calling upon Trusted Believers

Sometimes ordinary prayer is not enough. You need the community of faith to join your faith in trusting God to do what only He can do. You may have already been to the doctor. You may be taking medication. You may be facing nagging pain.

If your physical condition persists unresolved or worsens, then calling trusted believers of your church to pray for you is your right and responsibility as a child of God. God will use those who are seasoned in the church and in faith to pray with authority for you.

James gives us direction for these times. He describes concerted prayer by trusted believers for more serious sicknesses, severe conditions or longstanding ailments:

> Is any one of you sick? He should call the elders of the church to pray over him and anoint him with oil in the name of the Lord. And the prayer offered in faith will make the sick person well; the Lord will raise him up. If he has sinned, he will be forgiven.
>
> James 5:14–15

In some churches, this may specifically mean spiritual leaders such as pastors or elders or deacons. But depending on your situation and need, you may turn more quickly to other trusted believers. Perhaps your church leaders are uncomfortable praying in this way or even praying for healing at all.

You may have a spiritual counselor, friend or mentor who would be more than happy to pray for your healing. Or you may sense an anointing among some in your small group or ministry team, and you will urge them to pray for you. Or maybe they just care for you and are willing to stand with you and will pray earnestly for you. Someone in your small group may even discover and develop a spiritual gift of healing by praying for you!

Parents, who are God's spiritual covering over their children, should pray with authority for their sick children to be healed. But children can also pray for their parents, because God honors the simplicity of their faith! Spouses should pray for spouses. Friends should pray for friends. And when the answers have not yet come, they should enjoin other trusted believers within the community of faith to pray.

You trust these people to pray for you because they have a connection with God and they care for you. Plus, they will pray with authority. The Lord uses the prayers of these ordinary Christians in extraordinary ways. Calling these trusted believers to pray in faith is an exercise of *your* faith.

This confession of faith was recorded from the medieval Waldensian movement: "Therefore, concerning this anointing of the sick, we hold it as an article of faith, and profess sincerely from the heart that sick persons, when they ask for it, may lawfully be anointed with the anointing oil by one who joins with them in praying that it may be efficacious to the healing of the body according to the design and end and effect mentioned by the apostles."[1]

Some Pastoral Advice

In the churches I have served, I have trained elders to lead the way in praying for healing. But whatever your tradition, some should be trained to pray with authority. To help you, I have provided guidelines in Appendix 2: The Healing Ministry in the Church. Your sickness may be a door of providence to guide others into a new sphere of ministry!

Sometimes those with a spiritual gift of healing or other apostolic gifts pray for people at special meetings, and God may use their unique ministry to meet your need. If this opportunity is available to you, I would encourage you to take advantage of it. But I would also encourage you, if possible, to participate in these events with your pastor's blessing.

James intends God's healing to be a church family event. This seems to be the Lord's primary avenue. Jesus started only one organization and it is the Church. When an answer to prayer for healing is detached from the local church, the opportunity to bless the congregation is missed.

Prayer is the key. Your individual prayers or the prayers of others may unleash God's desire. The gifts of the Spirit exercised in a small or large group setting may make the difference. The role and ministry of prayer by the spiritual leaders could be a turning point.

Clinton Johnson was a young pastor in Iowa who had suffered for some time with a sacroiliac joint that would not stay in place. A chiropractor would work on it and get it in place, but within an hour or so it would pop right out. As Clinton was serving Communion one Sunday, God impressed upon him to trust the Lord to heal him. He asked the elders to pray for him right then and there. He trusted God to heal him and the Lord healed him! He has not had any problem with his sacroiliac since, for the past fifty years!

Your Faith Expression

Is it too hard to believe that God wants us to seek Him *first* for our healings? I wonder sometimes if we don't run to the medicine cabinet or call the doctor too quickly. I have noticed too often that people who are injured or ill seem to surrender all their power and their responsibility for their health to doctors and medicines rather than to God.

I wonder, too, if this is an expression of where their faith is really based. God certainly uses all these means, and I am not opposed to them. God uses doctors and hospitals, medical procedures and prescriptions. Yet often God calls us to seek Him first, not just for our spiritual lives, but for our physical wellbeing.

Practically speaking, you may have already spent significant time in prayer for your own healing. If the Lord has not yet healed you, then calling upon others to pray for healing *is* your faith expression.

These supportive believers may know you very well. But they may need to get better acquainted with you and your need. They may want to be assured that you definitely know the Lord as your Savior. They may ask you if you have any known sins to confess. They may prayerfully apply rules for discernment in knowing how to pray for you. If you have adequately prepared your heart, then you have nothing to fear. You are seeking God to meet your need through them. Your faith expression before God at this stage is merely to ask for their specific prayers.

If you want to follow a procedure, let me recommend these few steps. Ask the trusted believers to gather around you to pray for you. One can anoint your forehead with a drop of olive oil as a symbol of the outpoured ministry and working of the Holy Spirit. They can then pray in the name and authority of the Lord Jesus as the Holy Spirit prompts them to pray. In the mystery of divine healing, at least one will give utterance to the prayer of faith, if necessary God will forgive your sins, and the Lord Jesus Christ will heal your body.

Richard Baxter (1615–1691), English nonconformist leader, Presbyterian pastor and author of more than two hundred books, emphasized how this prayer of faith

114

brings healing to the sick. "When mercies of healing are granted in the very time of prayer, when there is no hope, is not this as plain as if God from heaven should say to us: 'I am at work.' How many times have I known the prayer of faith to save the sick when all physicians have given them up as dead?"[2]

A Climax of Faith

Your trust, of course, is placed in God to heal you. Yet you also recognize these believers as trustworthy channels of God's grace. While presenting the healing ministry in the Church, James also recognized these aspects:

> Therefore confess your sins to each other and pray for each other so that you may be healed. The prayer of a righteous man is powerful and effective. Elijah was a man just like us. He prayed earnestly that it would not rain, and it did not rain on the land for three and a half years. Again he prayed, and the heavens gave rain, and the earth produced its crops.
>
> James 5:16–18

These are people who know each other enough to be transparent about spiritual sins and physical needs. These are also people whose walk with God makes a difference. These are ordinary Christians, like Elijah who is "just like us," who believe in an extraordinary God who hears and answers prayer.

Imagine a collective group of praying friends, mature Christians, godly leaders, a supportive congregation— those who are spiritually responsible for you and care deeply for you—praying that God would do something great, something mighty for you. You called upon them to pray publicly or privately, large group or small. Combined with your personal preparation, an atmosphere of faith, hope and expectation is intensifying. You feel and smell the oil upon you, serving as a symbol of the outpoured Holy Spirit, stimulating your faith. The ones leading in prayer are inspiring your faith. Your faith is thus mingled and heightened with the faith of others in one grand climax of faith in the living and loving Lord Jesus Christ to heal *you*!

Clara Johnson had stomach cancer. They took her from Watertown, South Dakota, by ambulance about 450 miles to Mayo Clinic in Rochester, Minnesota. The surgeons operated on her, then sewed her back up, informing her that she had about six months to live. She returned to Watertown by ambulance and called for her pastor to come with some elders to anoint and pray for her to be healed. She lived for 25 years after that. When she finally died of old age, the doctors did an autopsy and found no signs of cancer. God had healed her completely! The Lord indeed is the Great Physician!

Reflections

1. Are you ready to call trusted believers of your church to pray for you as your faith expression?
2. Can you envision this time of special prayer of healing for you?
3. Do you see these fellow Christians as trustworthy channels of God's grace?

Prayer

God, I now call upon trusted believers as an expression of my faith in You to heal me. Praying friends, mature Christians, godly leaders and a supportive congregation further inspire my faith. I recognize them as trustworthy channels of Your grace as they pray in the name and authority of Jesus Christ. I affirm the anointing oil as a symbol of the outpoured Holy Spirit. Ultimately, my faith is in You. I believe in You.

13

Ask

Are You Ready to Ask God to Heal You Now?

In the second century, Irenaeus (ca.130–200), a church father, a bishop of Lyons in Gaul and later a martyr, wrote: "Others, still, heal the sick by laying their hands upon them, and they are made whole. Yea, moreover, as I have said, the dead even have been raised up, and remained among us for many years."[1]

The trusted believers you have called are ready to gather around you to pray for you. Your role is not to sit there passively, but to engage your faith actively. You are not a dead fish, but a living saint!

Jesus is with you, just as He promised, and He wants to hear from you. Could it be that until now you have not received because you have not asked? James wrote, "You do not have, because you do not ask God" (4:2).

You have decisively stepped out into new territory with no turning back. You are clear about your desire. You are standing firm on your convictions. You are serious about your commitment. *Now ask God to heal you.*

As these Christians surround you in prayer, let your heart pray in agreement with them. A spiritual transaction is taking place. You are committing your total self to God. You are reliving in your mind the Scriptures God gave you for this moment. You are claiming God's assurance to heal you by a definite act of faith now. Jesus said:

> "Ask and it will be given to you; seek and you will find; knock and the door will be opened to you. For everyone who asks receives; he who seeks finds; and to him who knocks, the door will be opened. Which of you, if his son asks for bread, will give him a stone? Or if he asks for a fish, will give him a snake? If you, then, though you are evil, know how to give good gifts to your children, how much more will your Father in heaven give good gifts to those who ask him!"
>
> Matthew 7:7–11

You are not simply accepting what God is giving; you are expecting something wonderful. You are not simply asking for something good; you are taking something great. *You are taking Christ as your Healer.* This moment is not a spiritual experiment that you hope will take effect sometime soon. You are taking the risen life of Jesus Christ for your specific need as a present reality!

Don't just hope that Jesus will heal you someday. Claim that your great Savior is touching you now. Believe that your loving Lord is beginning the work of healing in your body this very moment. See with your mind's eye the healing done.

You are exercising specific faith in God that is necessary to receive healing. You are applying a concrete belief that God is giving you healing. You are claiming special confidence in God that He is healing you now. Jesus assures you that He will do whatever you ask in His name and authority: "And I will do whatever you ask in my name, so that the Son may bring glory to the

Father. You may ask me for anything in my name, and I will do it" (John 14:13–14).

Faith is not a sleepy compliance that waits passively for something to happen. Faith is active receptivity that takes forcefully what God wants to give.

You have moved beyond the belief that God can heal you and that He has the power to heal you. You are claiming this specific blessing from the Lord. You are counting upon it to happen, confessing it to be true, considering the healing done and acting as though it is a reality. You are asking God to heal you!

Trusting God to Work

While by faith you are receiving your answer to prayer in the present, the now, you are also giving God time to work out the prayer's actual fulfillment in the way He sees best. As your friends conclude their prayers and say the final amen, you enter a new phase of trust. Trusting God is also active faith. As Abraham Lincoln (1809–1865) said, "Faith is not believing that God can, but that God will!"[2]

Your bold and bare kind of faith that *takes* God at His word, now *rests* with assurance in the arms of God's faithfulness. You are not depending on your feelings. You are not leaning on what you see, nor are you distracted by what you do not see. You are not allowing Satan to dissuade you from what God has told you in secret. Paul affirmed: "For no matter how many promises God has made, they are 'Yes' in Christ. And so through him the 'Amen' is spoken by us to the glory of God" (2 Corinthians 1:20).

As with your own salvation, you have come to a particular crisis point and taken a definite stand. You have placed a stake in the ground and pounded it in. You are saying in this deliberate act of united prayer: "This is what

God said. I believe it. I stand upon it." You trust God to work and to work out the fulfillment of His promises.

Trusting His Promises

While you realize that you cannot confine God's power to your expectations, you nonetheless pray in faith trusting God whatever the outcome. While advising people not to tell God *when* or *how* to heal them, Francis Mac-Nutt instructed:

> Healing is mysterious. The best we can do is bow down before the mystery that is God. When God chooses to reveal His mind, we can act with assurance. At other times, when we are in doubt about a particular case, the most honest thing to do is to admit our doubt and bow down before the awesome mystery of God's will.[3]

I like the way Norwegian Lutheran theologian Ole Hallesby (1879–1961) said it. He declared that we should pray something like this: "Lord, if it will be to your glory, heal suddenly. If it will glorify you more, heal gradually. If it will glorify you even more, may your servant remain sick awhile. And if it will glorify your name still more, take him to yourself in heaven."

At this step of your healing you are asking God with full faith to heal you for His glory. With confidence you are asking God to heal you in answer to specific prayer. Christ's assurance anticipated your delight in the Father's answer: "I tell you the truth, my Father will give you whatever you ask in my name. . . . Ask and you will receive, and your joy will be complete" (John 16:23–24).

You have asked. Others have prayed. Now you believe the answer is on the way. The Lord has heard you pray. Fully trusting in His promises, you rejoice in praise to God.

121

Reflections

1. How would you describe your faith for healing—definite or indecisive, specific or vague, active or passive, resolved or unsettled?
2. What does it mean to you to *ask* God for healing?
3. Where does trust fit in?

Prayer

> *God, I now step out solemnly, definitely and irrevocably in faith on Your Word and take Christ as my Healer. I believe You are giving me healing now as I actively and forcefully take it from Your hand. I also trust that You will work it out in fulfillment. I take You at Your word no matter what I feel or do not feel. I come to this definite point and cross it. I put down a stake and leave it forever. I claim Your truth and stand upon it. I ask You to heal me.*

14

Authority

Do You Need to Exercise Authoritative Faith?

Vera Mikelson has faced many challenges in life. She was born with cerebral palsy and could not walk until she was three. When she was four, the county nurse tried to put her away in an institution, but her mother said no. She started school when she was almost seven and went all the way through high school. But misfortune followed her: Her parents died when she was only nineteen. Eventually married, she continued to face one problem after another, including breast cancer, multiple surgeries and depression. The Lord had saved Vera when she was fifteen and her strong faith enabled her to develop in new dimensions. In spite of a lifetime of struggles, Vera remains a cheerful person.

As Vera's pastor, I visited her while she was in the hospital with pneumonia. I asked God how to pray for her and I sensed that He wanted to heal her pneumonia. It was Thursday. After praying with authority, I told Vera that I would see her in church on Sunday. She was there, released from the hospital Friday.

How do we know when to pray with authority? Where does authoritative faith fit? How does it work?

Simultaneous Happenings

Several things are taking place simultaneously while others are praying for your healing. Two things are assured. One, you are specifically and definitely *asking* God to heal you. Your faith is active. Two, you are also having a living *encounter* with the risen Christ. God meets you and brings you the blessing of His real presence.

Two things that you cannot control or demand, but *sometimes* happen, are these. One, the pray-ers may exercise authoritative faith. Through the Holy Spirit, they command the will of God to be realized in the name of Jesus. Two, you may experience further triggers of faith. You have some conscious sensation of God's presence or activity in your body. I will explain how authoritative faith works in this chapter and how to consider these triggers of faith in the next.

Authoritative Faith

What is authoritative faith? Authoritative faith is the kind of faith that commands the will of God to be done. It is not compelling or inducing God to do something He does not want to do. The work of the Holy Spirit acting through the faith of those praying characterizes this faith activity. They exercise divine authority by ordering the body to obey God's will and be healed.

George Fox (1624–1691), English founder of the Quakers or Society of Friends, described such an occasion:

> After some time I went to a meeting at Arnside, where was Richard Myer, who had been long lame of one of his arms. I was moved of the Lord to say unto him, amongst all the people, "Stand up upon thy legs," for he was sitting down. And he stood up, and stretched out his arm

that had been lame a long time, and said, "Be it known unto you, all people, that this day I am healed." Yet his parents could hardly believe it; but after the meeting was done, they had him aside, took off his doublet, and then saw it was true.[1]

Authoritative faith rises within people supernaturally when they have an overwhelming sense that God is at work. Don't be confused. You do not demand your will to be done. You are speaking God's will. And, remember, you can be overwhelmingly assured of what God's will is!

Especially when you believe the Lord has given you a word that He wants to heal you, share this with those praying for you. They may be timid in praying with authority and need this encouragement. *Your* faith may further inspire *their* faith and guide them in their praying.

This penetrating assurance of what God wants done rises up in those praying, and His will in them commands the release of His mighty power! Authoritative faith is what Jesus described in Mark 11.

> "Have faith in God," Jesus answered. "I tell you the truth, if anyone says to this mountain, 'Go, throw yourself into the sea,' and does not doubt in his heart but believes that what he says will happen, it will be done for him. Therefore I tell you, whatever you ask for in prayer, believe that you have received it, and it will be yours."
>
> Mark 11:22–24

Praying with authority begins with clear knowledge of what God wants. Have you definitely heard from heaven? If God wants a miracle, then pray for a miracle! Throw the mountain into the sea!

125

True Prayer

We can ask God for anything according to His will. Prayer is not persuading God to do what we want. It is not giving God marching orders. True prayer is discovering what God wants and then asking Him to do it. This He will then do! John wrote:

> This is the confidence we have in approaching God: that if we ask anything according to his will, he hears us. And if we know that he hears us—whatever we ask—we know that we have what we asked of him.
>
> 1 John 5:14–15

I know many times we lack the precise knowledge of what God wants. Just pray with the understanding and faith you do have, and trust God to do what only He can do. Authoritative praying is not necessarily loud praying or eloquent praying. It is praying with the confidence God gives.

You may decide to wait upon the Lord, lingering in His presence, until He gives you clear direction for healing prayer. Only do not assume that God does not want to heal you. Your goal is to pray on target. To hit the bull's eye, listen to the Lord.

At times, as we specifically ask the Lord for direction in prayer, He shows us how to pray and sometimes directs us to pray with incredible authority.

I made a hospital visit to a parishioner in his late seventies named Burton who had experienced a heart attack. While driving to the hospital, I asked God how to pray for him. I sensed clearly that this was not Burton's time to die. Some may call this a word of knowledge. When I arrived at his bedside in the ICU, I prayed for a quick recovery and that God would add years to his life. Burton was released from the hospital, back in church the following Sunday and claiming with tears in his eyes that his recovery was a miracle. God had answered the prayer that He had directed!

Delegated Authority

How does authoritative prayer work? Authoritative prayer is based on the principle of delegated authority through the name of Jesus. God wants to give what you seek and the prayer of faith lays hold of it. Christ delegated this authority and power to those praying through His name:

> "In that day you will no longer ask me anything. I tell you the truth, my Father will give you whatever you ask *in my name*. Until now you have not asked for *anything in my name*. Ask and you will receive, and your joy will be complete."
>
> John 16:23–24, emphasis added

Praying in Jesus' name means to pray in His authority, in His full person, with all that His name stands for. Identifying with Jesus in prayer on this level is to ask the Father just as if Jesus Himself were asking. Sometimes a conscious force of intense desire comes from the Holy Spirit through those praying. "God, do it and do it now in Jesus' name!"

In 1540, Lutheran reformer Friedrich Myconius (1490–1546) was very sick and about to die. He was so weak he could not speak, but he wrote a farewell letter to his dear friend Martin Luther (1483–1546), the German initiator of the Reformation. Luther sent back this response:

> I command you in the name of God to live because I still have need of you in the work of reforming the church. . . . The Lord will never let me hear that you are dead, but

127

will permit you to survive me. For this I am praying, this is my will, and may my will be done, because I seek only to glorify the name of God.

Myconius regained his strength and outlived Luther by two months!

Authoritative prayer is not lackadaisical praying or weak asking. Exercising delegated authority given to us by Christ is the confident and forceful taking from the heavenly throne what God wants to give. The Lord's Prayer teaches us to pray, "Your will be done on earth as it is in heaven" (Matthew 6:10).

Authoritative prayer frequently results in a demonstration of the Holy Spirit's power and a deeper connection with God. When Jesus walked upon the earth, the sick touched Him and became whole. As you reach out to touch Jesus today, He will make you whole and He will bring you into deeper union with God.

Faith That Takes

Authoritative faith, then, is believing God and His Word, and then taking with authority what He wants to give. You already believe that Jesus can and wants to heal you. You are simply expecting God to do now what He said He would do. You shut out doubt and fear and failure. You are looking for God to work and for God to get the glory. Overwhelmed with a sense of His unconditional love, you reach out to touch a living Savior. Positioned before God with a sense of unshakable confidence, you take healing from the hand of your divine Healer. You have a *faith that takes*.

Albert Simpson penned this simple refrain:

> There is healing in Jesus, healing for thee,
> Healing for all who believe and obey;

128

> There is healing in Jesus, healing for me—
> Jesus, I take Thee for healing today.[2]

Missionary Ian Hall tells the story of a woman named Cristina Ardeleanu, whom he met during a preaching crusade in a Romanian church in the city of Cimpulung. In September 1990, Cristina was in the hospital with an ectopic pregnancy. Before she even learned she was pregnant, the fetus had died and begun to decompose in her body. Doctors did not expect Cristina to live.

Ian and his wife, Sheila, went to the hospital to pray for Cristina, and God marvelously healed her. Still, in the doctors' attempts to save her life, they removed most of her uterus and one ovary. They told her that she would never bear a child.

Cristina's strength returned and within eight months she was back in church. Ian was holding another series of meetings there, and Cristina and her husband, Stefan, came forward for prayer. Accepting the medical diagnosis, they were hoping now to adopt. They asked, "Will you pray that God will give us a child?"

Ian began to pray, but suddenly he found himself prophesying: "In one year you will stand in this place holding a son born of your own body."

Sheila later asked him: "Why did you say that? You know she can't bear children. You've really put yourself out on a limb." Ian knew his predicament all too well. The words that came from his lips astonished everyone, including him!

During the next year Ian returned to that part of Romania, but Stefan and Cristina said nothing about a baby. Although troubled at first, in time Ian stopped thinking about the prophecy.

In May 1993, he was conducting services again in the Cimpulung church. The pastor announced that a baby would be dedicated and informed Ian that he was to pray for the child. Ian surveyed the audience, but he could not see anyone with a baby.

Then from the farthest corner of the church Ian saw a beaming Stefan and Cristina approaching the front. They were holding the son born to them six weeks earlier. As with Hannah of the Bible, the couple had received their promise from God—and they named him Samuel.[3] Authoritative faith takes.

Reflections

1. Have you ever experienced authoritative faith?
2. How would you describe Christ's delegated authority?
3. Even when you think others have not exercised authoritative prayer for your healing, how are you still trusting God to heal you fully?

Prayer

God, I acknowledge that at times You give authoritative faith that commands Your will to be done in the name of Jesus through the Holy Spirit. Indeed, as others pray for me they may experience an overwhelming sense of the power of the Holy Spirit upon them to command my body to obey Your will and be healed. I know it is not my will that demands healing. It is Your will that is being commanded through them. This heightened sense of faith takes forcefully and lays hold of Your desire. It asks just as if Jesus were asking, expects You to work Your will and results in a demonstration of Your Spirit's power. With confidence I reach out to touch and take healing from Your hand as my living Savior.

15
Sensations

*Are There Further Triggers of Faith
That God Gives?*

As I explained in the last chapter, two faith aspects that you cannot control or demand at this stage of prayer for healing, but *sometimes* do happen, are authoritative faith and triggers of faith. This is holy ground, full of mystery, a path we tread lightly. I want to discuss here the triggers of faith—the physical, emotional or spiritual sensations you *might* experience during or after people pray for you.

God is gracious to your psychological makeup. You are a whole person. You cannot separate your body and soul and spirit. They are interconnected to make you fully you. Thus, as you approach God, He can give sensations that help your feelings act like a trigger on a missile: They send your faith skyrocketing upward to God. Perhaps these feelings are only your response to God's nearness or activity. But they are nonetheless real.

You cannot expect these sensations or insist on them, but I believe that if they happen you can maximize them to your benefit. These conscious sensations of God's near presence or activity in your body are given for your encouragement.

It would be difficult to imagine Jesus handling His healing ministry in a perfunctory way without feelings. Consider the man He healed of leprosy: "Jesus reached out his hand and touched the man. 'I am willing,' he said. 'Be clean!' And immediately the leprosy left him" (Luke 5:13).

The leper was moved by that touch of compassion. He was moved by those gentle, affirming words, "I am willing." He was moved by that authoritative command, "Be clean!" That leper felt the touch. He heard the words. He felt and saw something happening to his body. Simultaneously the touch that healed his injured soul healed his leprous body. You, too, might feel the love of God embrace you as people pray for your healing. You will hear the words of those praying for you. You might feel and see something happening in your body.

Likewise, look at what happened to the crippled man whom Peter healed through the authority of Christ:

> Then Peter said, "Silver or gold I do not have, but what I have I give you. In the name of Jesus Christ of Nazareth, walk." Taking him by the right hand, he helped him up, and instantly the man's feet and ankles became strong. He jumped to his feet and began to walk. Then he went with them into the temple courts, walking and jumping, and praising God.
>
> Acts 3:6–8

This man could not stand, much less walk. He had to be carried to the Temple gate so he could beg. When this disabled man looked up at Peter's riveting gaze, he longed for some generous financial gift. Instead he received more than money. He was healed through the power of Jesus' name.

Suddenly he became aware of a strange, new strength in his legs and feet. In the time it took him to stand up, his tendons attached, his muscles grew and his sockets realigned. Life filled his legs. Instead of his legs collapsing, they now held him up!

First, he practiced standing. Then putting one foot forward, he tried to walk. Then even that was too ordinary. He began leaping in the air, bounding along, discovering everything that his limbs could never do. He entered the inner courts of the Temple like a giddy child—walking, jumping and praising God!

Possible Sensations

Some people feel nothing at all either during or after prayer. Simple faith in the Lord Jesus heals many of these people. Others have different sensations of varying intensity. They might feel something happening before others pray or during their prayer time or after prayer. Or they might experience sensations before, during *and* after prayer! Separate from or combined with the healing event, they feel God at work!

The experience of healing is similar to the experience of salvation. Some have dramatic conversions and others quietly undergo a transaction of their wills to God. Both are equally saved.

The healing event can include internal or external phenomena:

- A sensation of warmth or heat in the diseased area
- An infusion of light or being flooded with light
- A surge of power going through the body

- An involuntary trembling of limbs
- A sense of wellbeing and complete rest or peace
- An experience of deep joy or holy laughter
- A gripping inner conviction of being healed
- A supernatural experience such as a vision or hearing the voice of God speaking
- An overwhelming feeling of the divine presence
- A strong identification with Christ particularly in His sufferings
- A significant shift in perceptions where known or familiar things of God unexpectedly take on new meaning

Albert Simpson recorded the words of two individuals who experienced dramatic sensations. In the first, a woman was healed of heart disease. She stated: "[My pastor] came to me and anointed me with oil and offered the prayer of faith, and instantly, as quick as a lightning flash, shocks of Divine power went through me from head to foot, and it seemed as though a Divine hand was laid on my heart, and I was *healed*; every symptom left and never returned."[1]

In the other, a man was healed of severe headaches, which he described as something like brain fever. "I then requested prayer for immediate healing. . . . Directly I felt a power in my body similar to currents of electricity passing from head to feet, and in twenty minutes I sprang up and declared that the Lord had healed me . . . that I was well."[2]

Find the Balance

Some might be afraid that this discussion on sensations might lead seekers to focus on the experience of healing rather than on Christ the Healer. Someone may ask, "If sensations should not be my focus, then why mention them at all?" I mention them because, as I said above, they can happen and you need to take advantage of what God is doing in you. Let me allay your fears. Put this discussion in the proper focus. *Find the balance.*

Your purpose in the healing event is to get in contact with God. You are reaching out to touch Jesus. You are responding to the ministry of the Holy Spirit. Make sure that you are not looking for any emotional high or any conscious feeling or any physical sensation. *Choose and purpose and determine in your heart and mind that, feeling or no feeling, you will take God at His word for your healing.*

Then, if feelings come, let these sensations serve as further triggers of faith in the Lord to heal you. They might be evidence of God at work. Or they might be expressions of God's love and care for you. Above all, let your full focus be upon Christ. Feelings come and go, but Christ remains.

I recall the time a retired couple, Frank and Mary Mangano, who had served for years in the ministry, prayed for my sore back at their kitchen table. Unbeknown to them, my legs started shaking considerably underneath the table as they prayed! The Lord healed me that day in answer to their specific prayer. The trembling of my legs was a personal encouragement to me and a stimulus for faith that God was immediately answering their prayers for me.

Reflections

1. How might sensations bolster your faith?
2. Why can't you depend upon these sensations?
3. Are you willing to seek the Lord for healing with or without any conscious feelings or sensations?

Prayer

> *God, I realize that sometimes in Your grace, You give physical, emotional or spiritual sensations as additional triggers to bolster my faith. This strong sense of knowing or feeling might vary in intensity, might come anytime or might not come at all. Yet my goal is not to seek or look for some experience but to come in contact with You and be responsive to You. If some wonderful experience does occur, I receive it as encouraging evidence that You are at work in my body. Either way I give You thanks.*

16
Encounter

Is Your Authentic Faith Leading to an Encounter with the Risen Christ?

Climbing through the preparation phase and ascending into the fulfillment phase, you finally reach the summit. As trusted believers are praying for you, you encounter the risen and living Lord Jesus Christ! Healing is not an "it" to be taken. *Fundamental to understanding and experiencing divine healing is the knowledge that healing is an encounter with Jesus, the Lord of all.* The ancient promise is for you:

> He said, "If you listen carefully to the voice of the LORD your God and do what is right in his eyes, if you pay attention to his commands and keep all his decrees, I will not bring on you any of the diseases I brought on the Egyptians, for *I am the LORD, who heals you.*"
>
> Exodus 15:26, emphasis added

Flowing out of your intimate relationship with Jesus Christ, you have sought the Lord for healing. Framed within that love relationship with God, you now encounter Jesus Christ meeting your need. This divine-human relationship continues whatever the outcome. This divine encounter takes place within relationship.

Biblical Basis

How does all this work? *The biblical basis for physical healing is the death and resurrection of Jesus Christ.* Jesus died to redeem you completely—spiritually and physically. The death and resurrection of Christ were physical facts. His body died. His body was raised from the dead. When Jesus came out of the tomb, He had a real physical body. He did not drift out of the tomb as an ethereal vapor. Of course, His body had changed. His body is a resurrected body, but it is still a body.

Not only did Jesus give His body *for* you, dying for your sins so that God may forgive you, but He also gives His body *to* you. As your living Lord, He energizes and strengthens your body with His mighty power. Jesus gives you His strength. He gives you His vitality. He gives you His energy.

Paul explains how this works: "We are members of his body" (Ephesians 5:30). Paul emphasizes that as Christians we are "all members of one body" with one another (4:25), and we are members of the Church, the Body of which Christ is the Head (see 1:23; 4:12, 16).

In these verses, Paul is highlighting an important fact. He is emphasizing that we are part of Christ just as branches are part of the vine (see John 15). Just as the wife becomes part of the very life of her husband, so, too, we become part of the very life of Christ. Just as the husband nourishes and cherishes his wife, so, too, Christ imparts His own life to us in His body. We are connected to His body—spiritually, mystically, personally.

Paul further describes healing through the risen Christ by the Holy Spirit: "And if the Spirit of him who raised

Jesus from the dead is living in you, he who raised Christ from the dead will also give life to your mortal bodies through his Spirit, who lives in you" (Romans 8:11).

The same Holy Spirit who raised Jesus from the dead gives life to your physical body. His living body is given to you. God's power, the same power that raised Jesus from the dead, is infused into your worn out and suffering human body. You are exchanging your weakness for His strength, your disability for His ability, your diseased life for an impartation of the resurrected life of Jesus. Even while suffering, Paul anticipates how Christ's risen "life may be revealed in our mortal body" (2 Corinthians 4:11).

In the fourth century, a blind woman from Facidia, a small suburb of Rhinocorura, a city of Egypt, was brought to Hilarion (ca. 291–371) to be healed. Hilarion was an Eastern ascetic and disciple of Anthony the Great and one to whom Jerome traced the origin of monastic life in Palestine.

This woman who had been blind for ten years stated that she had spent all her money on doctors. Hilarion replied, "If what you lost on physicians you had given to the poor, Jesus the true Physician would have healed you." Then the woman cried out for mercy. Following the example of the Savior, Hilarion rubbed spittle on her eyes and she was immediately cured.[1]

Divine healing is the result of a real and personal connection with a real and personal Christ. Divine healing is Jesus coming to you, touching you with Himself, imparting His life to your body. Divine healing is the continuous flow of the indwelling Christ by the Holy Spirit into your whole being.

Resurrection Life

God imparts healing personally. As you reach out and touch your living Lord Jesus, His supernatural life extends to you spiritually and touches you physically. Once you touch heaven, heaven comes down. Glory fills your soul. Divine energy flows into your body. Divine healing is the impartation of the strength and life of Christ through the Holy Spirit.

God supernaturally imparts resurrection life to stimulate, quicken and revive that which is infirm, exhausted and weak. Ultimately, divine healing is not the mere restoration of ordinary, physical health. It is not the harmony or balancing of all aspects of body, mind and spirit. It is not the proper alignment of the natural powers of the body to heal itself, though we neither avoid nor deny any of these. It is a personal intervention of Christ.

One afternoon while playing on a wooden picnic table, four-and-a-half-year-old Jordon Wiens ran a splinter into his finger. Sobbing, he called his father, Gregory, at his office. Jordon said, "I want God to take the splinter out." His father told him that his mother could remove it easily. But Jordon wanted God to do it because when Mom takes a splinter out, it hurts. He wanted God to remove it "by Himself." When Gregory got home an hour later the splinter was still there, so he proceeded to remove it. He tried to teach Jordon that sometimes God uses others to do His work and sometimes it is painful.[2]

God certainly uses doctors, medicine, prescriptions, emergency rooms, hospitals and care centers as part of the healing process. These are gifts from God and can often be part of the larger healing team—though medical professionals may admit that the more they know about medicine, the more they realize how much they don't know. With wit Benjamin Franklin stated, "God heals, and the doctor takes the fees."[3]

But divine healing means primarily that the sick person is intrinsically brought into union with the body of the risen Christ and receives an impartation of His res-

140

urrection life. As God heals you, you can affirm with Paul, spiritually and physically, "I no longer live, but Christ lives in me" (Galatians 2:20). Physical healing thus becomes a foretaste of the future resurrection of the body.

Facing Unexpected Results

As you have an encounter with the risen Christ during the prayer ministry time and receive some blessing from God, you might also sense that the end result is going to be different from what you had wanted or expected.

For some an encounter with the risen Christ means supernatural grace for *physical healing.* For others it means supernatural grace for *active endurance.* Both kinds of dynamic encounter are grace filled!

John Packo is a noteworthy example of a pastor who took steps toward the healing of his cancer but has not been healed. He gradually understood that God was giving him strength to face the ordeal. He summarized the processing of his "healing" in twelve creative choices:

1. I did not choose cancer, but I choose to trust God for courage to cope with cancer.
2. Cancer is a divine appointment to receive Christ's miracle of His life into one's heart.
3. Since our sovereign Lord permits cancer for His glory and our spiritual growth, I will glorify God and grow.
4. Because Christ's death on the wondrous cross is the basis for divine healing, I choose His supernatural power to supplement my doctor's treatments.
5. I pick James' prescription administered by the elders of the local church, then leave the healing results to God.

6. If I select the wonders of modern medicine, I must be prepared to manage the not-so-wonderful side effects.
7. I practice positional thinking that produces power to live above tough circumstances.
8. When God withholds the miracle of instant healing, I humbly embrace His alternative of amazing grace that creates inner strength and a joyous disposition.
9. I love God who specializes in the miracle of turning cancer into my ultimate spiritual good of Christlikeness.
10. I dedicate my body to Christ and separate it from unhealthy eating habits, chemical abuse and overexposure to sun.
11. I accept death as the departure into heaven made possible by the resurrection of Jesus Christ from the dead.
12. I celebrate the wonder of life by filling my heart with the joy of worshiping Jesus.[4]

Even in suffering, Christ's resurrected life is revealed in your body. Paul stated:

> We always carry around in our body the death of Jesus, so that the life of Jesus may also be revealed in our body. For we who are alive are always being given over to death for Jesus' sake, so that his life may be revealed in our mortal body.
>
> 2 Corinthians 4:10–11

When the answer from God results in your healing, rejoice with celebration! When the answer from God calls for endurance, endure with patience! Your faith is still alive. An encounter with Christ has taken place. You are receiving grace. Your faith solution is not passive. Even your acceptance is a bold step of faith.

When faced with his own personal challenge that did not turn out as expected, Paul announced what God said and how he responded: "But he said to me, 'My grace is sufficient for you, for my power is made perfect in weakness.' Therefore I will boast all the more gladly about my weaknesses, so that Christ's power may rest on me" (2 Corinthians 12:9).

Faith and healing present a very subtle and complex relationship. I wish it were simpler, but it is not. As your faith gropes toward God, you know you have no power to control the outcome. Yet whenever faith is evident—whatever the end results—authentic faith elicits an encounter with the risen Christ.

Miracle Encounter

Not many conversion stories make it to the pages of the *Wall Street Journal*, but Dr. Marvin Overton's did. A June 6, 1994, article by Robert Johnson shows how true it is that when a person accepts Christ, all things become new.

Dr. Marvin Overton is considered to be one of the most skilled brain surgeons in the nation. In 1992 he began attending a small church in Burnet, Texas, and had a spiritual awakening. About the same time, he began suffering severe, lingering pain in his abdomen. X-rays eventually revealed cancer. Several days after the diagnosis, however, the tests showed nothing, and Overton has felt fine ever since. The Lord completely healed him. The healing crystallized his spiritual awakening as a genuine born-again experience.

Before his conversion he was a skeptic and a rationalist who believed in the power of science. Now, says the *Journal*, Overton "has more answers than questions,

143

a granite certitude about the mind, the brain, and the soul."

Before his conversion he was, by his own description, cold hearted. Overton said: "I was a good surgeon, but I was coarse. I couldn't shed a tear. My attitude [toward patients] was 'tough.'" Now he writes notes to friends, notes containing encouraging quotes from Scripture, and he cares enough about patients to ask those scheduled for surgery, "If something goes wrong, are you comfortable that you know God and that you'll go to heaven?"

Before Overton's conversion, wine was his idol. He wasn't an alcoholic, but he did own one of the finest wine collections in the country. He said, "I worshipped the god Bacchus. . . . I was an excellent heathen." After his conversion, he sold his wine collection, giving much of the proceeds to charity.

Before his conversion, Overton was a Fort Worth socialite. Now he is a leader in his small-town, blue-collar church in Burnet, Texas. He goes door-to-door telling others about Christ.

Michael McWhorter, chair of the American Association of Neurological Surgeons science board, said: "Who are we to say a miracle didn't happen? Something changed his life." When a person becomes a fully devoted follower of Jesus Christ, all things become new.[5]

What a powerful example of encountering the risen Lord Jesus Christ! God saved his life *and* healed his body! What is the Lord doing in you?

Reflections

1. Do you agree or disagree with this statement: "Healing is primarily an encounter with the risen Jesus"? Why or why not?

2. How would you describe what is taking place spiritually when trusted believers are praying over you?

3. Which requires more grace—healing or endurance?

Prayer

God, in this moment I now encounter the risen Jesus—for healing is not an "it" to be taken but an encounter with Jesus! I affirm that divine healing means becoming united with Christ's risen body and is the impartation of His strength and life through the Holy Spirit! I confirm that divine healing is Your supernatural divine power infused into my human body, renewing my strength and replacing the weakness of my suffering human body by Your life and power. I attest that divine healing comes through the life of the resurrected Christ who rose from the dead bodily and is a foretaste of the future resurrection of my body. I bear witness that divine healing comes via the work of Your Holy Spirit. This same Jesus who healed by the Holy Spirit while on earth is still the same for me today! God is real, Jesus is alive and the Holy Spirit is working in power!

After Prayer for Healing

What comes next? Following your personal preparation for healing and an encounter with Jesus through prayer for healing, you now enter new territory—the ongoing process of healing and health. In this completion phase you will find key aspects to help you continue to grow in the wonderful mercy of Christ our Healer.

Do

*Are You Believing and Acting
As Though God Has Healed You?*

Thirty-one-year-old Lawrence Dent was ambitiously shingling a chicken house. Time was ticking away and he was going to have to rush to catch his train home. So instead of climbing down the ladder, he foolishly jumped off the roof . . . twelve feet to the ground. Nothing bothered him right away. But after the train ride, serious pain caught up with him. When he got back home that evening, he could not stand the agony.

The next day the doctor informed Lawrence that his top two vertebrae were crushed. After ten days in the hospital in a stretcher sling, he was put into a body cast from his neck to his lower hips. Three days later he went home uncomfortable and irritable. The cast was too constricting for this energetic family man.

Only nine months earlier, Lawrence had followed the Lord in water baptism. Though he had made a childhood profession of faith in Christ, Lawrence was enjoying the blessings of a fresh and full commitment to his Savior. Now this had to happen. He could not afford to take time off work: He had a family to provide for. The cast was to stay on for eight more weeks. He was getting more and more cranky.

Two weeks later after praying together, Lawrence and Betty, his wife, went to church for special prayer. The Rev. Sack Palmer and visiting preacher Rev. John Mcarthy prayed for him, and Lawrence knew he was healed! He could feel it. Though he had faith in his well-known and well-credentialed doctor, Lawrence took a hunting knife and some vinegar and cut the cast off! For him this was the right thing to do. Keeping the cast on would only cause him to doubt his healing. Obedience strengthened his faith. His life took another leap forward in understanding Jesus as Sanctifier, Healer and Coming King. God had indeed healed him, for Lawrence has had no problem with these vertebrae for more than forty years. He believed and acted *as though* God had healed him.

Continuing Faith

God has brought you to a summit of faith regarding divine healing. Now He wants you to discover that faith for healing is both a specific act and an ongoing activity.

You have claimed healing. Now you want to keep it. How? By continuing. Continuing in faith. Continuing to keep right with God. Continuing to count on God to take care of you. Continuing to believe that God will honor His Word. Continuing to receive new life from Him.

God will help you to claim His truth, to mature in holiness, to grow in faith, to be established in hope and to believe in His love.

Just as happens when you are training a new muscle and feel soreness as it develops, so you may also be aware of the energy it takes to develop your faith further at this level. As much as possible, you now want to act *as though* the Lord has healed you. This next step of faith is rooted in the New Testament ministry of healing through Jesus and the apostles. Faith is more than something you believe; faith is something you do or act upon.

The following five stories are taken from the four gospels and the book of Acts. Notice the words I have placed in italics.

Story #1

Matthew records this event of Jesus healing a man with a shriveled hand: "Then [Jesus] said to the man, 'Stretch out your hand.' So *he stretched it out* and it was completely restored, just as sound as the other" (Matthew 12:13).

As an expression of his faith, this man had to stretch out his hand. Jesus did not grab it and yank it out. A command from God is the guarantee of the power to do it.

Story #2

Mark tells us that when Jesus healed the paralytic who had been lowered through an opening in the roof, Jesus asked: "Which is easier: to say to the paralytic, 'Your sins are forgiven,' or to say, '*Get up, take your mat and walk*'?" (Mark 2:9).

The man was not supposed to lie there and expect to be wafted up on angels' wings. He had to get up. He had to pick up his mat. He had to shove one foot out in front of another. He had to walk. He had to carry his mat all the way home! "He said to the paralytic, 'I tell you, get up, take your mat and go home.' *He got up, took his mat and walked out* in full view of them all. This amazed everyone and they praised God, saying, 'We have never seen anything like this!'" (Mark 2:10–12).

151

Story #3

Luke describes the story when Jesus healed ten men who had leprosy. Jesus told them to act *as though* God had healed them. In this instance, Jesus did not approach the lepers who were calling out to Him. He did not reach out and touch them. He did not even say, "You are healed!" He did this: "When he saw them, he said, 'Go, show yourselves to the priests'" (Luke 17:14). This was the scriptural procedure for a leper who had been cured by God. The priest, serving as a kind of health inspector, would examine the individual and certify that a cure had taken place.

Jesus was asking these ten men to act *as though* God had already healed them. What a test! Yet the Scripture adds that as they obeyed what Jesus told them to do, so it happened! "And *as they went, they were cleansed*" (Luke 17:14).

Story #4

John records Jesus' order to the man born blind: "'Go,' he told him, 'wash in the Pool of Siloam' (this word means Sent). So *the man went and washed, and came home seeing*" (John 9:7).

The blind man had to follow the directions of Jesus. He had to go and wash his eyes. This may seem an unkind order at the outset. Why not just heal him right then and there? Why force him one last time to feel his way along in the darkness of his unseeing eyes? But Jesus knew what He was doing. As a faith expression, this man had to obey what Jesus asked. Then after he went and after he washed, he came home seeing!

This pattern modeled by Jesus—calling people to activate their faith, to act *as though* God had healed them—continued with the apostles.

Story #5

When Paul and Barnabas were preaching in Lystra, they met a man crippled in his feet who was lame from birth and had never walked. Luke wrote: "He listened to Paul as he was speaking. Paul looked directly at him, saw that he had faith to be healed and called out, 'Stand up on your feet!' At that, *the man jumped up and began to walk*" (Acts 14:9–10).

Paul did not reach out to the invalid and pull him up. The man himself jumped up and began to walk.

This sampling of stories is enough to underscore the fact that some concrete expression of your faith is necessary. Jesus and the apostles commanded the sick and infirm to do something. "Stretch out your hand." "Get up, take your mat and go home." "Go, show yourselves to the priests." "Go wash in the Pool of Siloam." "Stand up on your feet." All were acts of obedience.

Albert Simpson expressed well this principle of obedience in healing:

> What though you feel so weak and faint?
> He can your will with strength endue,
> New faith and courage breathe within
> And work in you to will and do.
>
> Reach out to meet His quickening touch;
> Take up your bed, arise and stand;
> And pressing through to meet your Lord,
> Stretch forth your hand, stretch forth your hand.[1]

When you stretch out your hand at God's command, and upon the Lord's promise take your stand, Christ will make you whole. *As-though* faith is a step of obedience.

153

Faith reaches up and takes divine life from God. The consistent pattern of faith at this phase of healing is acting *as though* or *as if* God has healed and is healing you.

A Word of Caution

Let me also add an important caution concerning this dimension of faith: Do not be tempted to grab this faith principle alone and not take into account preparation of heart and mind, or counsel and prayer from mature Christian friends, or a clear directive from God. Some people have, for instance, stepped on their eyeglasses, claiming to be healed of poor eyesight, only to replace them later. Some diabetics have stopped their insulin shots, only to go into insulin shock and have to be rushed to the hospital. Some have even died because they chose to rely solely on spiritual methods rather than seeking medical assistance. There are dangers and consequences of taking steps that are ill-advised, presumptuous and foolhardy.

True, the processes of faith go beyond the boundaries of rational logic and empirical evidence. Yet faith is not irrational, nor is it unreasonable. After prayer for healing, you do not abandon your mind. You do not automatically disregard all medical indicators. Be practical. Use common sense.

If you have not yet seen specific results to prayer and are unsure of how to move forward in the belief that God has healed you, get counsel from godly Christians. Look for further confirmation from still other Spirit-filled Christians. It is not a lack of faith to continue medical treatments until your doctor has confirmed your healing; it is not an insult to God to persist in sensible remedies until you have felt or seen marked improvement in your body. God may well use these means to heal you. Above all, pray that God will give you direction.

154

Please note that apparent "failure" to receive an immediate healing does not shake true faith, and people whom the Lord has not healed do not necessarily have less faith. You are not retreating from faith by following good sense and mature Christian counsel

Following Clear Directions

But to the degree that you feel the freedom, you can begin ignoring the symptoms. You have already stepped out boldly to build your faith for healing; now take practical steps that exhibit your faith. You can begin disregarding uncomfortable feelings and nagging impressions. You can begin attempting to do what was previously impossible. You can continue to claim and trust the Lord for the reality of your healing.

Consider doubts and fears as temptations to be overcome. Refuse to listen to these nagging voices. Resist the notion that God has not healed you. Reckon symptoms as foreign to yourself. Like taking a breath of fresh air, begin to breathe in new life and health and strength from God.

You have intentionally prayed for healing; now stop thinking about your sickness. Stop fearing it. Even stop talking about it with others. These are not psychological gimmicks. These are honest and courageous expressions of your faith. You are intentionally detaching yourself from your infirmity and standing firm in faith.

Glance Versus Gaze

How does this kind of faith work? Healing does not occur because you are exercising faith in faith. You are healed because you are expressing faith in God. Faith elicits healing, but it is not faith that heals. God heals and faith receives that healing.

When God is truly at work, you will realize the expression of your faith as fact in your physical body. Faith counts upon healing and considers it done as *a finished reality* before you see it, feel it or experience it.

Jesus described this *as-though* kind of faith: "Therefore I tell you, whatever you ask for in prayer, *believe that you have received it*, and it will be yours" (Mark 11:24, emphasis added). The author of Hebrews also summarized this kind of faith: "Now faith is being sure of what we hope for and certain of what we do not see" (Hebrews 11:1).

Don't say that you don't see anything happening or that you don't feel any different. *Keep on believing* even when every evidence is to the contrary. At this point your faith *is* the evidence of your healing!

I know that when we are sick, it is often difficult to focus on the God of healing and health. Your inner life may be consumed with your physical condition and dominated by your struggle for health. Sickness and evil are almost hypnotic. Yet deliberately taking your mind off your physical condition and consciously placing it onto God are vital.

While your *glance* may be on your condition, let your *gaze* be upon God! Don't be mesmerized with your feelings. Don't get caught up with your anatomy. Don't watch the ups and downs of your medical situation. Get out of yourself. Keep busy with God and give yourself in serving others. Go on to the next thing you are supposed to do. Perhaps as you are busy with God and for God, He will be working in you.

Faith Keeps Believing

Duane Miller is a Christian who kept on believing what God's Word says about healing even when he did not see it in his own body. Duane was teaching his Sunday school class from Psalm 103 at the First Baptist Church in Brenham, Texas, on January 17, 1993. He had retired prematurely from the pastorate three years earlier because of a virus that penetrated the myelin sheath around the nerves in his vocal cords. This virus reduced his speech to a raspy whisper. The story of his heroic struggle was the subject of several Christian magazine articles.

With a special microphone resting on his lips, Duane taught his class that day, reaffirming his belief in divine healing and declaring that miracles had not ended with the book of Acts. At times the people could barely understand his weakly spoken words of faith. Yet a miracle happened when he reached verse 4—how the Lord "redeems your life from the pit." He said, "I have had and you have had in times past pit experiences."

When he said the word *pit*, his voice and his life changed. The word was as clear as a bell, in contrast to the imperfect enunciation of the preceding word *past*. He paused, startled. He began again and stopped. He said a few more words—all in a clear, normal tone of voice—and stopped again. Then the class burst out in shouts of joy, astonishment and weeping. God completely healed Duane as he was declaring the truth of Psalm 103![2]

When God has healed you, He will make it clear to you. You will know it and God will get the glory.

Reflections

1. How do you see faith for healing as an ongoing activity?
2. What are some things you should stop doing?
3. What are some faith things you should start doing?

Prayer

*God, I understand that faith for healing is both
a specific act and an* ongoing activity. *While
avoiding the dangers and consequences of ill-
advised, presumptuous and foolhardy actions, I
am believing and acting as one healed. I take my
mind off myself and my condition and place it
upon You. I am choosing to ignore symptoms
and suffering, trusting the actuality of my
healing. As an expression of standing firm in
faith, I now stop thinking about, fearing and
talking about my sickness. I am focusing on
staying busy with You and for others. I will keep
believing You in spite of immediate evidence to
the contrary, considering my healing as a
finished reality before I see it. As a concrete
expression of my faith, I* do something, *perhaps
even attempt to do what was previously difficult
or impossible. I am continuing to keep right
with You, continuing to acknowledge that You
will take care of me and will honor Your Word,
and continuing to receive new life from You.*

158

18
Trials

Are You Prepared for Trials of Faith?

A man found a cocoon of the emperor moth and took it home to watch it emerge. One day a small opening appeared and for several hours the moth struggled but could not seem to force its body past a certain point.

Deciding something was wrong, the man took scissors and snipped the remaining bit of cocoon. The moth emerged easily, its body large and swollen, the wings small and shriveled. He fully expected that in a few hours the wings would spread out in their natural beauty, but they did not. Instead of developing into a creature free to fly, the moth spent its life dragging around a swollen body and shriveled wings.

The constricting cocoon and the struggle necessary to pass through the tiny opening are God's way of forcing fluid from the body into the wings. The "merciful" snip was, in reality, cruel. Sometimes the struggle is exactly what we need.[1]

No matter how remarkable the specific healing event may have seemed when seasoned Christians prayed for you, it is only a part of the process. After prayer for healing and while "doing" what God may be calling you to do, be prepared for trials of faith. Peter stated: "Dear friends, do not be surprised at the painful trial you are suffering, as though something strange were happening to you" (1 Peter 4:12).

Your symptoms may linger. Your condition may not disappear immediately. You may face delays and setbacks physically or spiritually. Discouragement, doubt and fear may come. Yet these trials serve only to test and strengthen your faith.

In fact, the testing of your faith may come in direct proportion to the intensity of God working in you! Be assured, if God has brought you this far, He will take you all the way through. God will confirm your faith with His answer. Indeed, "the Lord knows how to rescue godly men [and women] from trials" (2 Peter 2:9).

Three keys in facing these trials are confronting temptation, understanding time concerns and persevering in faith.

Confronting Temptation

You may face the kind of internal questioning that diminishes faith: "How will I know if I am healed? What if this isn't God's time to heal me? What if I didn't fulfill all the conditions for healing? What if I have asked God for too much?"

As with all temptations, Paul encourages us: "No temptation has seized you except what is common to man. And God is faithful; he will not let you be tempted beyond what you can bear. But when you are tempted, he will also provide a way out so that you can stand up under it" (1 Corinthians 10:13).

You may feel like Oscar Wilde who said, "I can resist everything except temptation."[2] Do not let discouragement, doubt or fear about your healing control you.

160

Resist these temptations. Remind yourself of the truths of God's Word. Rebuke the enemy of your soul and body. Remember that God provides a way out.

Ask yourself if the temptation agrees with the Word and the Spirit! *Does this thought line up with God's truth? Is this what the Holy Spirit has been saying to me about my healing?*

If not, then say no to the temptation! Submit yourself to God. If this thought does not agree with God's message to you in the Word or by the Spirit, dismiss the thought immediately. Don't have anything to do with it. If it keeps coming back, keep saying no. "I do not have to do that, think that, believe that lie. I don't live there anymore. No means no."

If the temptation keeps plaguing you, kick the tempting suggestion out! If it still will not let go, resist Satan and command him to leave. Talk back to the devil. Kick the devil out. Use the Word of God with authority. Swing the sword of the Spirit. Speak out the specific word of God that the Holy Spirit rises up within you to speak out.

Jesus won over temptation. He lifted up truth. He said no. He resisted. He overcame. He found a way out. God came to meet His need. *And God will provide a way out for you.*

Treat discouragement, doubt and fear about your healing by setting your will against them. You choose to believe and obey. You decide not to be discouraged, not to doubt, not to fear. Faith is not something you feel. Faith is something you believe. Faith is something that prompts you to take action. English Christian mystic Julian of Norwich (ca. 1342–1416) wrote:

> He said not
> "Thou shalt not be tempted;
> thou shalt not be troubled;

161

thou shalt not be distressed,"
but He said,
"Thou shalt not be overcome."[3]

Understanding Time Concerns

Sometimes the concern of time weighs heavily and challenges your faith. Perhaps you expected an instantaneous healing. That has been the experience of some Christians. Yet God may sovereignly choose another plan. D. Martyn Lloyd-Jones said: "It is a fundamental principle in the life and walk of faith that we must always be prepared for the unexpected when we are dealing with God."[4]

Your healing may occur over a short or long period. The speed at which God works can be immediate or delayed. God's pace in healing you can be gradual or a process of stages. The results of God's answer can be complete or partial. God may choose to heal you supernaturally without medical intervention, or He may choose to work through doctors and hospitals. When God heals, God heals in a variety of ways. The following chart helps visualize this.

When God Heals

God's Timetable	Short	Long
God's Speed	Instantaneous	Delayed
God's Pace	Gradual	A Process of Stages
God's Answer	Complete	Partial
God's Instrument	God Alone	God through Others

My father, Sam, received the ministry of prayer for his diabetes. His condition improved and stabilized, but he still has diabetes. He received a partial healing.

My father also prayed that God would not let his diabetic condition be an impediment to his pastoral ministry. God told him that if he lived a disciplined life, his request would be answered. It has been!

The words "They will get well" (or recover) from Mark 16:18 could imply a healing process. However fast or slow God is working, your healing is from Him and He should get the credit. God works in different ways at different times. Whenever and however you recover from an illness, consider yourself divinely healed. That way God gets the credit as the supreme healer of your body. Even the next breath you take is a gift from God. French surgeon Ambroise Paré (1517–1590) had his life motto inscribed above his chair in the Collége de St-Cosme: "Je le pansay et Dieu le guarist" (I treated him, but God healed him).[5]

Persevering in Faith

Runner's World tells the story of Beth Anne DeCiantis' attempt to qualify for the marathon in the 1992 Olympic Trials. A female runner must complete the 26-mile, 385-yard race in less than 2 hours, 45 minutes to compete at the Olympic Trials.

Beth started strong but began having trouble around mile 23. She reached the final straightaway with just two minutes left in the qualifying time. Two hundred yards from the finish, she stumbled and fell. Dazed and disoriented, she stayed down for twenty seconds. The spectators yelled, "Get up!" The clock was ticking: less than a minute to go.

Beth Anne staggered to her feet and began walking. Five yards short of the finish, with ten seconds to go, she fell again. She began to crawl, the crowd cheering her on, and crossed the finish line on her hands and knees. Her time? Two hours, 44 minutes, 57 seconds—3 seconds under the qualifying standard.[6]

The writer of Hebrews reminds us to run our race with perseverance and never give up: "Therefore, since we are surrounded by such a great cloud of witnesses, let us throw off everything that hinders and the sin that so easily entangles, and let us run with perseverance the race marked out for us" (12:1).

True faith holds on to God tenaciously until the full answer comes and accepts the answer in whatever form it takes.

Reflections

1. What trials of faith are you facing?
2. How are you overcoming temptations of discouragement, doubt and fear?
3. How does the concern of time relate to your situation?

Prayer

God, if my symptoms linger, grant me grace to overcome the temptations of discouragement, doubt and fear. I set my will against them. I choose to believe and not to be discouraged, not to doubt, not to fear. I acknowledge that healing may occur over a short or long period—instantaneously or delayed, gradually or in a process of stages. It may be complete or partial. When I do not feel any faith, I choose to believe until the full answer comes, and I accept healing in whatever form it takes.

19
Abide

*Are You Continuing to Draw Life
from the Risen Christ?*

This announcement was seen on a church bulletin board: "No healing services Sunday due to the pastor's illness." Even the best prayers sometimes don't work!

What if God says not yet? What if God says no? How do you continue to draw life from the risen Christ?

When God Says Not Yet

What if you have prayed for healing but nothing seems to happen? What if no immediate answer to prayer comes? What if you still have questions? What if God says, "No, not yet. Wait a while. Keep asking"?

Reviewing earlier steps you have taken may be fitting. Praying again until a clear answer comes from God may be appropriate. With a humble heart, you may be asking, "God, what am I yet to learn?" Simultaneously, you are trusting God and still believing the answer is on the way. Even while the Lord's answers may be unclear, you are cultivating a deeper love for God. Your heart is abiding. Jesus said:

> "I am the vine; you are the branches. If a man *remains in me* and I in him, he will bear much fruit; apart from me you can do nothing. . . . If you *remain in me* and my words remain in you, *ask whatever you wish, and it will be given you.*"
>
> John 15:5, 7, emphasis added

In 1929, J. C. Penney learned an important lesson about God's care. That year he was critically ill and had gone to the Kellogg Sanitarium in Battle Creek, Michigan, for treatment. One night, while in deep despair, he wrote farewell letters to his wife and son, telling them he did not expect to see the dawn. But he survived the night, and the next day he had an experience that changed his life.

He testified: "When I awoke the next morning, I was surprised to find that I was still alive. Going downstairs, I heard singing, 'God will take care of you.' Going into the chapel, I listened with a weary heart to the singing, the reading of the Scripture lesson, and the prayer. Suddenly—something happened. . . . I felt as if I had been instantly lifted out of the darkness of a dungeon into warm, brilliant sunlight. I felt as if I had been transported from hell to paradise. I felt the power of God as I never had felt it before. I realized that God with His love was there to help me."[1]

Do not despair. Delays may take place. God isn't finished with you yet! Remain. Dwell in Christ. Live in His love. Stay in His Word. Walk in His Spirit. Abide in the vine!

When God Says No

But what if God says no? What if you have persistently asked God for healing, but you get progressively worse?

166

What if God says, "No, I love you too much. I have a different plan"?

We affirm that the Kingdom of God is "already here" as a present reality—Jesus came to earth, died and rose from the dead that we may be healed. But the Kingdom of God is "not yet" fully come—we do not always know why God does not heal every person all the time. I could give a dozen unsatisfying answers. Sometimes a Christian's life work is completed and God calls that person home to heaven. Sometimes God shortens a life because of disobedience. Although the idea is overused and often abused, sometimes those who are sick do lack faith.

Faith for healing is not just taking all the necessary steps. It goes beyond believing correct doctrine. It goes beyond submitting to a ritual of anointing with oil. It goes beyond agreeing with the prayers of others. It goes beyond acting as though God has healed you. True faith is clear and distinct and doubts not that God intends to heal. Real faith personally takes God now, presses through the crowd and touches the garment of Christ. Still, God sometimes answers no.

Divine healing goes no further than the promise of God. God does not promise that you will never die. Even Lazarus, whom Jesus raised from the dead, later died. God only promises that you will fulfill your number of days and complete your life's work. God assured us through Moses that "your strength will equal your days" (Deuteronomy 33:25).

As your days, so will your strength be. If you continue to suffer, the sovereign God will give you grace in your suffering. God will be glorified even in your weakness (see 2 Corinthians 12:9–10). Even in death itself, God will give you grace to triumph.

Once when he was to preach at the University of Sydney in Australia, John Stott lost his voice. He wondered before God, *What can You do with a missionary who has*

167

no voice? He had come to the last night of an evangelistic campaign. The Christian students had booked the big university hall. A group of them gathered around Stott, and he asked them to pray as Paul did, that this thorn in the flesh might be taken from him. But they went on to pray that if it pleased God to keep him in weakness, he would rejoice in his infirmities in order that the power of Christ might rest upon him.

As it turned out, Stott had to get within one inch of the microphone just to croak the Good News of Christ to his audience. He was unable to use any inflection of voice to express his personality. It was just a croak in a monotone, and all the time the Christian students were crying out to God that Christ's power would be demonstrated in human weakness.

Stott honestly had to say that there was a far greater response that night than on any other night of the campaign. He has been back to Australia ten times, and on every occasion somebody has come up to him and said: "Do you remember that night when you lost your voice? I was converted that night."[2]

Continue to Draw Life

Whether God says not yet or no, whether God delays or denies your healing, your faith remains active. *You continue to draw life from the risen Christ.* The Lord will give new life to your mortal body through His Spirit who lives in you (see Romans 8:11). Paul also wrote from personal experience: "I have been crucified with Christ and I no longer live, but Christ lives in me. *The life I live in the body, I live by faith in the Son of God,* who loved me and gave himself for me" (Galatians 2:20, emphasis added).

Just as you began looking in faith to God for healing, keep fixing your eyes on Jesus, the author and perfecter of your faith (see Hebrews 12:2). The God who has brought you this far will bring you all the way through without faltering or He will bring you all the way home without stumbling (see Jude 1:24). Peter said that a day is coming when you will have it all, life healed and whole. Meanwhile, you *"through faith are shielded by God's power* until the coming of the salvation that is ready to be revealed in the last time" (1 Peter 1:5, emphasis added).

God's power guards you from assaults. God's keeping grace carries you along. After totally yielding your whole life to God to use for His glory and service, after believing without doubt in the assurance of His Word for healing, He calls you to abide in Christ for your physical life. Live there.

Whatever the outcome, you come to a place of what some classical devotional writers like Ignatius Loyola (1491–1556), founder of the Society of Jesus, called "indifference." That means you are completely open and utterly receptive to God's yes or no. Like a balance at equilibrium, you are ready to go up or down as God desires. You relinquish all personal interest for the greater glory of God. Whether you live or die, whether God heals you or you suffer, you live in your body by faith in Jesus. Either way you win! God calls you to depend upon Him personally. God calls you to draw your strength daily from Him.

In the center of Bath, England, a stone marker honors the city's medicinal waters that have blessed so many people. Grateful citizens had the monument inscribed with the following words: "These healing waters have flowed on from time immemorial. Their virtue is unimpaired, their heat undiminished, their volume unabated. They explain the origin, account for the progress, and demand the gratitude of the City of Bath."

169

How like the grace of God! It, too, is an endless stream of freely flowing, health-giving water that never cools and never fails. *Continue to draw life from the risen Christ.* Paul stated that Christ is your very life: "For you died, and your life is now hidden with Christ in God. When Christ, who is your life, appears, then you also will appear with him in glory" (Colossians 3:3–4).

Reflections

1. If the Lord has not healed you yet, what might He be saying to you?
2. What can you do if God says wait?
3. What can you do if God says no?

Prayer

God, while still believing the answer is on the way—the posture of "waiting"—I continue to abide in Christ for my physical life and draw my strength moment by moment in personal dependence upon You. My inquiring mind reviews earlier steps to see if I missed anything. My trusting heart asks You what I am yet to learn. I may learn that Your answer is no, for You do not promise that I will never die, only that I will fulfill my number of days and complete my life's work. With expectant faith I most certainly ask for my full length of days and the completion of my life's work. I acknowledge Your sovereignty to extend grace in healing or in suffering, in health or in death. Even when healing is delayed, my faith remains active in continuing to draw life from You, my risen Savior.

20

Providence

Are You Trusting Christ
Even if He Has Not Healed You?

The only survivor of a shipwreck washed up on a small, uninhabited island. He prayed feverishly for God to save him. Every day he scanned the horizon for help, but none seemed forthcoming.

Exhausted, he eventually managed to build a rough hut out of driftwood to protect him from the elements and store his few possessions. But then one day, after scavenging for food, he arrived home to find his little hut in flames, the smoke rolling up to the sky. The worst had happened. Everything was lost. He was stung with grief and anger.

He cried out, "God, how could You do this to me!" Early the next day, however, he was awakened by the sound of a ship approaching the island. They had come to rescue him. The weary man asked the crew, "How did you know I was here?"

They replied, "We saw your smoke signal."[1]

When things are going bad, we can easily get discouraged. We do not always see things the way God sees them. You may be wondering: *Why is a chapter on what to do if Christ has not healed me or apparently chosen not to heal me included in a book on healing? Doesn't Jesus heal? Doesn't this undo everything already said?*

While I affirm that the message of healing is clear, I also acknowledge that the mystery of healing is real. I think a complete look at the complexities of divine healing is honest. Your little hut burning to the ground may be the very smoke signal that summons the grace of God.

Paul's Testimony

A fascinating testimony is found in the life of Paul.

> To keep me from becoming conceited because of these surpassingly great revelations, there was given me a thorn in my flesh, a messenger of Satan, to torment me. Three times I pleaded with the Lord to take it away from me. But he said to me, "My grace is sufficient for you, for my power is made perfect in weakness." Therefore I will boast all the more gladly about my weaknesses, so that Christ's power may rest on me. That is why, for Christ's sake, I delight in weaknesses, in insults, in hardships, in persecutions, in difficulties. For when I am weak, then I am strong.
>
> 2 Corinthians 12:7–10

Christian scholars do not agree on what was Paul's thorn in the flesh. *The Quest Study Bible* summarizes the diversity of viewpoints:

> Some suggest that it was a spiritual problem (anxiety, sexual temptation or perhaps guilt). Others see it as a physical ailment (headaches, epilepsy, malarial fever, a speech impediment or even eye problems). Still others speculate that it referred to Paul's frequent persecutions.[2]

172

This thorn in the flesh, this messenger of Satan, could also have been a spiritual problem of pride or more literally an evil spirit. What I want to emphasize, however, is not what it was but *how Paul dealt with it.* He prayed about this thorn in the flesh three times, perhaps in a pattern similar to Christ's in the Garden of Gethsemane. While God may not remove your thorn, He does want to change you. Instead of chafing under the thorn, you can glory in it—not in the thorn itself but in the occasion to see the display of God's grace.

Perhaps the first time Paul sought the Lord and God said no, he may have wondered: *Did I hear God right? Maybe God said wait. If so, I want to keep asking. Maybe God said no, but that wouldn't make sense in light of all the assurances He has given me. I'd better ask again.*

The second time he prayed through his condition, God's answer may have been more clear and definite, but Paul may have thought: *Okay, I think God is definitely saying no. But how can this be? God usually says yes to meet the needs and cries of all His children. I'd better ask the Lord one more time just to make sure.*

After he asked God one last time, asking the Lord why He did not remove this thorn, no doubt, Paul concluded: *Now I know and understand what God is uniquely saying to me. God's answer is sure and certain, and here's why—God will be glorified in my weakness! Okay, then. I will take pleasure in my weakness, so Christ's power will be more visible to others.*

I think that if you are unsure of God's answer, with Paul, ask again until you know for sure. *Seek to be healed until God either heals you or tells you why He is not going to.* God says no for a reason.

Ask Him to show you a verse of Scripture to verify it. When my father was not totally healed of his diabetes, the Lord gave him Romans 8:23—"Not only so, but we ourselves, who have the firstfruits of the Spirit, groan

173

inwardly as we wait eagerly for our adoption as sons, the redemption of our bodies." God was telling him that he would find full healing at the resurrection.

Discerning His Hand at Work

Sometimes when God does not answer our prayers, we do not understand why until much later. That was the experience of Kathy Healy. At age fifteen she became seriously ill and could not seem to get better. After a five-year period during which she had endured three major surgeries and more than 350 days in the hospital, the doctors finally uncovered her problem—celiac axis compression syndrome, a rare disorder with the artery near the heart. Elderly people most often experience this disease.

Kathy's Christian family and friends began to pray that God would perform a miracle. In Kathy's own words, here's what happened: "I prayed for healing, too. The Lord gave me a peace about my sickness. I never doubted it came for some reason. While I never doubted, I did wonder if I would ever find out that reason."

Twenty years later she did. It came in the form of her nine-year-old daughter. She was ill, in severe pain, and lost fifteen pounds in three short weeks. In that condition she would most likely not live many more weeks. Kathy suggested to her doctors that her daughter might have a rare disorder in her artery near her heart. While they thought this would be highly unlikely—because it could not happen in a child—the doctors did look into it and found the same condition Kathy had. In fact, they had to admit it was something they never would have thought to look for. They had never even heard of it!

Although Kathy's daughter still deals with daily pain, she is with the family and able to thrive. Now her daughter wonders why the Lord let her go through this, but she, too, trusts God's greater purpose for her life.

Leith Anderson comments: "Kathy's story is probably repeated a million times a day. Someone prays for something that God denies and then uses his 'wrong answer' to accomplish something else—perhaps a generation or even generations later."[3]

When you have given yourself totally over to God, you begin to see His hand behind all the situations in your life. You try to learn what God is teaching you through every circumstance however desirable or difficult. Since God is a God of love even when you do not understand Him, you trust Him to guide you even through darker paths and always into spiritual maturity. Even misfortune, illness and spiritual struggles can bear fruit in your life that God can turn into what is good for you. That is the message of the often-quoted Romans 8:28: "And we know that in all things God works for the good of those who love him, who have been called according to his purpose."

Abandonment to Divine Providence

Jean Pierre de Caussade (1675–1751), a French ascetic writer, popularized the phrase "abandonment to divine providence." When God has not healed you, you abandon yourself to God's providence. You relinquish your desires and demands to God. This abandonment to God is neither a passive patience nor a regretful resignation. *Your abandonment is an active acceptance, a willing embrace, an obedient response to the Lord.* Jesus submitted to the divine will in the Garden of Gethsemane: "Father, if you are willing, take this cup from me; yet not my will, but yours be done" (Luke 22:42). In your darkest moments you, too, can affirm, "Father, I know that if

175

You want, You can change this. You can heal me. But ultimately *I want what You want!*"

Thus, in your abandonment to divine providence, you conform lovingly to the divine will as the best way. You are resolute about continuing to follow the teachings of God's Word as the right path. You obey God's authority for He has the words of eternal life. You accept the ups and the downs of your physical condition in your everyday life as from God.

Submitting your will to God's will can be very difficult. Even Jesus had to repeat His prayer of surrender in the Garden three times (see Matthew 26:36–39, 42–44). Submission to God's will is something you have to renew constantly. Like Jesus, you may need to affirm and reaffirm, "Nevertheless, not my will, but Yours." Oswald Smith wrote:

> Into the cross of Jesus
> Deeper and deeper I go,
> Following thro' the garden,
> Facing the dreaded foe;
>
> Drinking the cup of sorrow,
> Sobbing with broken heart,
> "Oh Savior, help! Dear Savior, help!
> Grace for my weakness impart."[4]

Some misunderstand abandonment to mean that you are giving up and acquiescing to evil. No. You hate sickness, suffering and death. *Still, you make every effort to change what you can change, and at the same time, you accept what you cannot change.*

Choose to see how God can use all things, the pleasant and the unpleasant, for His glory and your good. Embrace God's "good, pleasing and perfect will" in wealth or poverty, joy or distress, health or illness, life or death (see Romans 12:2). God's thoughts and ways are higher than and beyond ours (see Isaiah 55:8–9). And "give thanks in all circumstances, for this is God's will for you in Christ Jesus" (1 Thessalonians 5:18).

In the center of a main street in Enterprise, Alabama, stands one of the strangest monuments in the world. It is a memorial to an insect! Handsomely carved in stone is the likeness of a boll weevil. Many believe that divine providence was involved in the circumstances that led to the erection of this unusual statue.

In early plantation days almost everyone in the community raised cotton. But as the years rolled on, a serious pestilence infested the area in the form of a small beetle that punctured the boll of the plant. As a result, it became almost impossible to bring a season's growth to maturity.

George Washington Carver, along with several other scientists, became deeply concerned about the situation and began intensive studies to see if any substitute crop could be grown in that part of the country. Raising peanuts was the answer, for they could be planted and harvested with very little loss. In time, cotton gins were forgotten in that region and it became known as an outstanding peanut center of the world. Soon the farmers' profits far exceeded what they had earned from their best cotton yield. In the end, they realized that the destructive boll weevil they had feared had actually triggered the research that brought them prosperity.

Personal Transformation

The assurance that God is present and active in all that happens in every moment of your life will become a great consolation to you and an opportunity for personal transformation. Your teachable response before God to

177

everything that comes your way ensures that you are growing in Christian character and in the knowledge of our Lord Jesus Christ. What begins as an unconditional surrender to God and His ways continues as a wholehearted willingness to see God in all the ups and downs of your physical challenges.

When you are perplexed or dismayed by difficulties, the Lord God will remind you, "This is my doing" (1 Kings 12:24). We often fail to see God's hand. In the same spirit as Mary, the mother of Jesus, abandon yourself to divine providence, saying: "I am the Lord's servant. . . . May it be to me as you have said" (Luke 1:38). By faith, see beyond all your cares and concerns to the Lord of love who reigns in power. Through your yieldedness to the Lord of circumstance and situation, God is painting a picture of Christ on the canvas of your life.

Let me further illustrate by considering the prayers of Jesus in the Garden of Gethsemane:

> Then Jesus went with his disciples to a place called Gethsemane, and he said to them, "Sit here while I go over there and pray." He took Peter and the two sons of Zebedee along with him, and he began to be sorrowful and troubled. Then he said to them, "My soul is overwhelmed with sorrow to the point of death. Stay here and keep watch with me."
>
> Going a little farther, *he fell with his face to the ground and prayed, "My Father, if it is possible, may this cup be taken from me. Yet not as I will, but as you will."*
>
> Then he returned to his disciples and found them sleeping. "Could you men not keep watch with me for one hour?" he asked Peter. "Watch and pray so that you will not fall into temptation. The spirit is willing, but the body is weak."
>
> *He went away a second time and prayed, "My Father, if it is not possible for this cup to be taken away unless I drink it, may your will be done."*

178

When he came back, he again found them sleeping, because their eyes were heavy. *So he left them and went away once more and prayed the third time, saying the same thing.*

Then he returned to the disciples and said to them, "Are you still sleeping and resting? Look, the hour is near, and the Son of Man is betrayed into the hands of sinners. Rise, let us go! Here comes my betrayer!"

Matthew 26:36–46, emphasis added

While committed to be the Savior of the world, Jesus would face overwhelming emotional and spiritual suffering and physical pain. He naturally turned to His Father for help. Through His prayers He was letting go of those things that would hold Him back from doing God's will. Praying the same thing three times suggests that Jesus was taking progressive steps in prayer.

1. *Realization.* Jesus' first expression in prayer was an outburst of grief. He realized the full impact of His mission. He shuddered in the chill of death's dark shadow. His only refuge was prayer. His longing for support from His companions was left unfulfilled while they slept.

   You likewise, in *realization*, feel the impact of what God seems to be asking of you by not healing you, trusting that God will see you through.

2. *Release.* In the Garden of Gethsemane Jesus faced two choices—save His own life and lose us, or lose His own life and save us. He wanted to do the will of His Father, so He accepted His calling to die for us. The Father's will became His will.

   In *release*, you let go, trusting that the Lord wants His best for you—body, mind and spirit, now and forever.

179

3. *Resolve.* Finally like tempered steel, Jesus gathered strength from His Father and left all His anxiety with Him.

In *resolve*, you boldly affirm your desire to honor God in your body as God gives you a rising sense of grace and power.[5]

Realization, release, resolve. Pray through these three interior movements of abandoning yourself to divine providence when you conclude that God has *not* healed you. Like Jesus, repeat them when necessary. *If you have never struggled with doing God's will, then you do not know what it is.* After the struggle, doing God's will is delightful. But yielding to God's will for your body in this way, especially when God says no, can be difficult. Follow the example of Jesus in the Garden. Abandon yourself to divine providence and let Him transform you!

Living with Pain

Elizabeth Mittelstaedt, living with her husband, Ditmar, near Frankfurt, Germany, is the editor of *Lydia*, a German Christian magazine for women.

In *Today's Christian Woman*, Elizabeth wrote how some years ago, she spent five hours in a dentist's chair for what was supposed to be a routine dental procedure. She was left, however, with a severely damaged nerve in her jaw. As a result, shooting pain—worse than a severe toothache—pulsated constantly on the right side of her face.

To rid herself of this excruciating pain, Elizabeth traveled from one doctor to another for six months. But nobody was able to prescribe something to ease her torment and despair.

Finally, a doctor at the Mayo Clinic in Minnesota told her: "Mrs. Mittelstaedt, there's nothing more that can be done to repair the damage or relieve your pain. You'll have to live with it."

When Elizabeth returned home to Germany with this news, she felt discouraged and deeply depressed. Medical records bear out that many people who suffer with the same problem resort to suicide. She, too, felt death was the only escape. But as a Christian, she could not believe this was what God wanted.

Still, the constant pain took its toll. She felt hopeless, with nothing left to hang on to. One day, during her morning walk, she crossed a small bridge near Frankfurt. Looking down at the flowing river below she was tempted to jump. But she concluded that the water was too shallow to drown in. Then the thought came to her: *Don't worry. It's stony down there. You'll hit your head and die anyway.*

At that moment, Matthew 4:5–7 came to her mind. She recalled in a similar way how the devil had unsuccessfully tempted Jesus to jump from the highest point of the Temple. So she said: "No, I am *not* going to jump. I am going to trust God."

Elizabeth began telling God what she was most afraid of—living in pain. Then she recalled that Jesus says we should not worry about tomorrow—that He gives us strength for one day. She resolved, *Somehow, I'll make it through the day.*

As she looked out over their town and saw the beautiful, steepled, fairy-tale homes with flower-filled window boxes, white picket fences and clean-swept sidewalks, she realized that behind this perfect façade were thousands of Europeans struggling with the aftermath of two World Wars—broken marriages, depression, guilt, loneliness and crushed hopes. She felt the Lord tell her: *Elizabeth, these women are suffering like you are today, and they want to give up. But their pain is different—it's emotional.*

181

She no longer felt so alone in her pain. Suddenly she was filled with a desire to encourage those women. That morning, the vision for a Christian women's magazine in Europe was born, which now is printed in Germany, Romania, Hungary and Serbia.

More than a decade has passed since that day by the bridge. Instead of shutting the door on her life, she opened a window to God for more than one million European women who subscribe to or buy her *Lydia* magazine off book stands in the streets and in the supermarkets. The magazine also goes into thousands of doctors' offices where it brings hope and encouragement to those who are not only sick in body but also often "wounded" in their souls. Its message is simple—hope and encouragement can be found through faith in Christ and His Word.

So many people turn to God for the first time when they face physical crises in their lives. Every year Elizabeth receives hundreds of letters telling how God has ministered to readers through the pages of *Lydia*. Letters like this one came from a new mother: "Thank you for the explanation about the value of life. Through reading *Lydia*, I decided to keep my baby and I have named her after you." Another wrote, "Thank you—this magazine is my only friend." Another gave the best news of all: "I want to share with you that I have given my life to Jesus Christ. Thank you for the good articles." When Elizabeth reads these responses, her heart is thrilled and a deeper healing takes place within her.

Yes, pain is still her companion—but it is no longer as overwhelming as it once was. When she searched God's Word for encouragement and comfort, she came upon Psalm 34:19: "Many are the afflictions of the righteous: but the LORD delivereth him out of them all" (KJV). The words to the left of the colon describe her circumstances—and the words to the right give her real hope for the future. But she has learned that when she hangs onto the colon in the middle—waiting in faith on God's promise and offering her pain to Him—it is never wasted.[6]

English poet William Cowper (1731–1800) wrote:

> God moves in a mysterious way
> His wonders to perform;
> He plants His footsteps in the sea,
> And rides upon the storm.
>
> Deep in unfathomable mines
> Of never-failing skill
> He treasures up His bright designs,
> And works His sovereign will.
>
> Blind unbelief is sure to err,
> And scan His work in vain;
> God is His own interpreter,
> And He will make it plain.[7]

Jesus says to you: "You do not realize now what I am doing, but later you will understand" (see John 13:7). Acknowledge that God is sovereign. Commit yourself to the Lord. Wait patiently for Him to act. Seek professional medical attention if necessary. Realize that it may not be God's will for you to be healed. Ask the Lord for faith, patience and wisdom. Pray that your circumstances will work out for the glory of God. *Abandon yourself to divine providence.*

Reflections

1. Are you sure God has said no?
2. What might be God's answer to your question, Why? Have you asked God for a Scripture to verify it?
3. How can you abandon yourself to divine providence?

Prayer

Father God, today I actively accept and willingly embrace Your will. I know You haven't abandoned me, and I abandon myself to You and Your divine providence. I know that if You want, You can change my situation and heal my body, but I want what You want. I pray with Christ, "Not my will, but Yours." I realize what this might mean, and I trust You to see me through. I release and let go of the whole thing, for I know that You want what is best for me. I resolve to honor You no matter what, believing You for the grace of healing or the grace to endure suffering. Be glorified in my body in whatever way You choose.

21
Living

After Your Healing,
Are You Living a Changed Life?

Starr Daily began running with the wrong crowd when he was a teenager. He served three prison sentences, the last one for burglary. While locked up, Starr plotted a prison riot. His plan was discovered and he was placed in solitary confinement. Lying on the cold floor, memories of his parents praying for him came to mind. He remembered his fear of death and his dreams that Jesus would release him from that fear. Compelled by love, Starr asked Christ into his life.

After his release from solitary confinement, Starr grew in Christ's love and became a model prisoner. He discovered that evil is not only the opposite of good, it is the opposite of life. If you spell out the word *evil*, the reverse is *live*.

When the Lord reverses the course of evil, you begin to live. When God has healed you, you have "crossed over from death to life" (John 5:24). You live now in health and healing to the glory of God!

Here are two pieces of pastoral advice for living in health and healing. The first is drawing life from Christ and the second is living for God's pleasure in practical ways.

Drawing Life from Christ

For you God has said yes. "Yes, and I thought you would never ask! Yes, and here's more!" You have received healing. What do you do next? Where do you go from here? Is that all there is? Is healing the goal?

I probably do not need to tell you to celebrate your healing! Like the crippled man healed through Peter, without instructions, you may feel like "walking and jumping, and praising God" (Acts 3:8)! Go ahead—laugh aloud and shout for joy! Give God praise! Enjoy the gift of heaven! Revel in your newfound healing! Bask in the glory of the Lord! Linger in His presence! Celebrate!

Healing is a gift from God that came out of your relationship with Him. After your healing, you continue growing in that relationship. After the emotions fade, you continue living in health and healing by continuing to walk with God. You "look to the LORD and his strength; seek his face always" (1 Chronicles 16:11). You may wonder with humility, "Why me? Why did Jesus heal me?"

Please consider this: The loss of your healing is possible. After healing an invalid, Jesus gave him a warning: "Later Jesus found him at the temple and said to him, 'See, you are well again. *Stop sinning or something worse may happen to you*'" (John 5:14, emphasis added). Jesus challenged the man to give up his sin. Continuing in it could bring a worse fate, perhaps even worse than his former physical handicap.

After experiencing the power of God in healing, the Lord challenges you now to live a changed life! If your attitude expresses the notion, "Now that I've got what I want from God, I can do whatever I please," then you are in

186

danger of losing your healing. An arrogant attitude like this is very much against the spirit of grace. Grace is a gift; it must not be abused.

Your desire should be to maintain a consistent prayer life in communion with God. Your aim is to avoid any psychological or spiritual obstacles that could disrupt your dependence upon Him. Why? You want to retain your healing, of course, but you really want more than that. You want to live in health. *You want the continuous impartation of the divine life into your body.* For ongoing health and healing you want the divine life of Christ flowing ceaselessly into your mortal body (see Romans 8:11).

Renewed Strength

How does that work? How do you receive a continuous impartation of the life of Christ? How do you maintain divine life for your body? This is not complicated. You receive this divine life in a quiet, normal way. *It is as natural as breathing.* Soon after receiving your healing from the Lord, for instance, it is natural to look heavenward spontaneously and thank God for His indescribable gift.

The secret of ongoing health is found in taking God's strength for your body continuously . . . in living upon God's life . . . in experiencing not only divine healing but divine health as well . . . in drawing renewed strength day by day through the Word of God . . . in receiving divine life when you participate in the Lord's Supper. You are walking with the living Christ in His resurrection life. You are growing in physical and spiritual strength.

The psalmist wrote: "They go from strength to strength, till each appears before God in Zion" (84:7). The new strength you have is not from yourself but from Christ. Place yourself in Him. Lean on Him. Draw energy from Him. *Your very life is Christ!* This risen Lord Jesus Christ

After Prayer for Healing

is above you, beyond you and yet within you, giving your body renewed strength.

This is God's promise to you: "Do not fear, for I am with you; do not be dismayed, for I am your God. *I will strengthen you* and help you; I will uphold you with my righteous right hand" (Isaiah 41:10, emphasis added). Spiritual, physical and emotional strength come through breathing out your old life and breathing in new life in God!

Spiritual Breathing

Breath is a powerful image of life. One person says, "Oh, I can't catch my breath." Another says, "With every breath you should be thankful!"

Breathing is also a powerful image of the Holy Spirit's movements. In Genesis, God breathed into Adam the breath of life. In Ezekiel, the blowing wind of God's Spirit revived the dead. After Jesus' resurrection, He imparted the Holy Spirit to His disciples by *breathing* on them: "And with that he [Jesus] *breathed* on them [the disciples] and said, 'Receive the *Holy Spirit*'" (John 20:22, emphasis added).

The disciples *felt* the breath of God upon them. They responded to this movement of the Spirit. They positioned themselves to wait until the fullness of the Spirit came on the Day of Pentecost.

You can live for weeks without food and a few days without water. But you cannot live more than a few minutes without air. Likewise you cannot live spiritually without the breath of the Holy Spirit.

Albert Simpson understood spiritual breathing— breathing out your old life and breathing in new spiritual life. With every breath, you exhale your life of sin and self and inhale the life of the Holy Spirit. He wrote this poem, "Breathing Out and Breathing In."

188

I am breathing every moment,
Drawing all my life from Thee.
Breath by breath I live upon Thee,
Blessed Spirit, breathe in me.

I am breathing out my own life
That I may be filled with Thine,
Letting go my strength and weakness,
Breathing in Thy strength divine.[1]

Simpson was describing what we could call a discipline of spiritual breathing. Breathe *out* your sinful desires, stress and sorrows. Breathe *in* righteousness, peace and joy in the Holy Spirit. It is like installing a hot air furnace in a home. You have to make a vent for the old air to go out and a vent for the fresh air to come in. Otherwise it won't matter if you have the thermostat cranked up all the way. The building will be as cold as a barn.

Learn this art of spiritual breathing—breathing out your old life and breathing in new life in the Spirit. *This is vital for your spiritual life; it is equally important for your physical life—breathing out the unhealthy elements of your body and breathing in divine life for health and strength for each new day.* "Lord, I breathe out my pains and weaknesses. I breathe in Your healing and strength."

Divine Health

Even when bad things happen to good people, since we have no guarantee of perfect health, we can still realize some dimension of divine life and wholeness. If an ailment returns or you face another sickness, then you have a fresh opportunity to seek the Lord and perhaps learn some new lesson. The spiritual life is a continuous journey of faith.

189

God may heal you on one occasion and not in another. Even when an answer does not come as hoped, God is still your strength. As the psalmist says, "My flesh and my heart may fail, but God is the strength of my heart and my portion forever" (73:26).

Strive constantly to climb higher and higher in order to live in God and with God and for God. Any time the going seems easier, better check to make sure you're not going downhill!

What am I trying to say? *Beyond divine healing is divine living, and beyond divine healing is divine health.* When those trusted believers prayed for you, the Lord lifted you onto a higher spiritual plane. Now you must choose to live there *always*. The overflowing life of God is for your whole human life—body, mind and spirit—as you live for God's glory and pleasure.

In this place of health you receive not only divine touches of healing but also the divine life that comes from your union with the Lord Jesus. In brief, divine health looks like this:

- When you prayed for healing, you surrendered your body to God, just as you did with your soul when you came to Christ. When you gave your life to God, Jesus became your Savior. When you gave your body to God, Jesus became your Healer.
- Now, through a definite act of your will, accept and receive Christ as your strength. Take Him for your health instead of relying on your own natural health.
- Next, cultivate the habit of depending upon Him constantly for strength. Recognize the Holy Spirit in you to quicken your physical body.
- Finally, learn to feed upon the Lord. Learn to drink in His life. Learn to breathe in His Spirit.

Don't despair. Don't give up. Wait on the Lord. Learn.
Lean. Breathe. Eat. Walk. Trust. Depend.

He gives strength to the weary and increases the power
of the weak. Even youths grow tired and weary, and
young men stumble and fall; but those who hope in the
LORD will renew their strength. They will soar on wings
like eagles; they will run and not grow weary, they will
walk and not be faint.

Isaiah 40:29–31

Living for God's Pleasure

Alongside these spiritual emphases, do not neglect
to live for God's pleasure in practical physical ways.
Since your body is the temple of the Holy Spirit, you
have a holy responsibility to take care of your body.
Don't think that you can abuse your body and then keep
running to God again and again for healing. Discipline
your body by eating right, getting proper exercise and
getting adequate rest. Control the use of your eyes,
your ears, your tongue. Keep your whole being set
apart for God.

Stand-up comic Rich Ceisler makes this all-too-
common observation: "Joined a health club last year,
spent four hundred bucks. Haven't lost a pound. Apparently, you have to show up."[2]

Theologian, author and futurist Leonard Sweet in fun
records "Ten Commandments for an Unhappy Life."

1. Thou shalt wear a grim expression at all times, and
   thou shalt hold thy body in a stiff and rigid posture,
   and exercise thy muscles as little as possible.
2. Thou shalt never get too close to anybody.
3. Thou shalt stuff and store all thy feeling in thy
   gut.

191

4. Thou shalt put aside play, and shalt inflict upon others that which was once inflicted upon thyself.
5. Thou shalt remain logical and analytical whenever possible.
6. Thou shalt go to as many "all-you-can-eat" buffets as thou canst.
7. Thou shalt not party.
8. Thou shalt not take a vacation.
9. Thou shalt expect the worst in all situations, blame and shame everyone around thyself for everything, and dwell on the feebleness, faults, and fears of others.
10. Thou shalt be in control at all times, no matter what.[3]

I guarantee that if you follow these ten commandments, you will be *unhappy*!

Manage your stress for Jesus' sake. Follow the doctor's orders for Jesus' sake. Choose to be happy for Jesus' sake. Enjoy your life in God. "Do not grieve, for the joy of the LORD is your strength" (Nehemiah 8:10). God is, indeed, over all.

A young sculptor worked painstakingly on the statue of an angel. When the great Michelangelo came to view it, the artist hid nearby and waited to hear the master's comment. Michelangelo looked intently at the sculpture with breathless suspense. At last he said, "It lacks only one thing." Hearing this, the young artist was heartbroken. For days he could neither eat nor sleep. A friend became so concerned for him that he went to Michelangelo to ask what the statue lacked. The master replied, "It lacks only life; with life it would be perfect."

Some Christians are like that statue. They maintain an admirable appearance. They live exemplary lives. They are respected citizens who are active in charitable functions. They are faithful members in their churches.

They are born again. But they lack one thing—they do not live for the pleasure of God.

As the Spirit of God breathes life continuously into your body, mind and spirit, live for the pleasure of God. *Live in Christ and in His health and healing!*

Reflections

1. What is the difference between divine healing and divine health?
2. How can you receive divine life for your body *continuously*?
3. What practical measures do you need to follow through on?

Prayer

God, I want to receive continuously the divine, resurrected life of Christ for my health and healing—receiving both divine touches for healing and divine life for health. I want the Spirit of Jesus to flow into my whole being ceaselessly and become to me as natural as breathing. *If sickness comes, if bad things happen to good people, I know this will be a fresh opportunity to receive grace and learn some lesson. I surrender my body to You and take Christ as my physical strength. I choose to keep my body holy and feed upon You as I eat and drink in Your life. I also take responsibility to exercise common sense in nutrition, stress management, physical fitness, a healthy diet and proper rest and relaxation. You are over all!*

22

Purpose

*Are You Using Your New
Strength and Health for God?*

Some years ago, when trains were the predominant mode of travel, a pastor made a long overnight trip to Texas to attend a convention of Mexican Christians. While he was there, he received word that his wife had suddenly been stricken with a serious illness. He was urged to return at once. Immediately he hurried to catch the first train home. During the long, sleepless hours of the night his heart was filled with anxiety. The next morning the conductor handed him a telegram, saying, "It must be important, for it was specially relayed to us at the last station."

As he took the yellow envelope, the minister replied, "I believe it is bad news, perhaps even a death notice." Then with deep emotion and trembling hands he slowly opened it. As he read the words, tears filled his eyes. He was overwhelmed, not with sorrow but with joy.

This was the message: "Mexican Convention in session all night. Prayed for you and your wife. She will get well!" When he arrived home, he found that she had begun to improve from the hour he had left the meeting. Although the pastor and his wife were unaware of it at the time, both of them had been upheld by the power of prayer in a fellowship of love!

God Healed You for a Purpose

God's children often say after the Lord healed them: "God healed me for a purpose. God has something for me to do." Divine healing is given to us so we can fulfill the purposes of God. Paul connected his physical strength with his spiritual service:

> I thank Christ Jesus our Lord, who has given me strength, that he considered me faithful, appointing me to his service.
>
> 1 Timothy 1:12

> But the Lord stood at my side and gave me strength, so that through me the message might be fully proclaimed and all the Gentiles might hear it.
>
> 2 Timothy 4:17

Healing is a sacred act of God. Through healing you have entered a sacred trust. God healed you so that He can use you more effectively in Kingdom work.

You are a recipient of God's grace. Now the Lord wants you to become a giver of grace in service to others. Your rejuvenated physical life is to be used for God's pleasure. Ask yourself before God: *With this new strength and health, where does the Lord want me to serve Him and others now?*

John also connected physical health and spiritual vitality in his prayers: "Dear friend, I pray that you may enjoy good health and that all may go well with you, even as your soul is getting along well" (3 John 1:2). God healed you for a purpose.

God Did Not Heal You for Yourself

In contrast, God did not heal you so you can squander your new strength and health on yourself. Receiving the grace of health does not give you permission to "go on sinning" (Romans 6:1). The Lord had no intention for you to use your renewed body for selfish pleasures and unrestrained living. Paul prayed: "May God himself, the God of peace, sanctify you through and through. May your whole spirit, soul *and body* be kept blameless at the coming of our Lord Jesus Christ" (1 Thessalonians 5:23, emphasis added).

Hezekiah is an example of one who made a tragic mistake in this regard. The story, told in Isaiah 38–39, describes how this king of Judah became ill and was at the point of death. Isaiah the prophet told the king that he would not recover and to set his house in order. Even so, Hezekiah prayed for healing and the Lord gave him a sign that he would indeed be healed: The sun's shadow on the stairway would go *backward* ten steps.

After God miraculously healed him and added fifteen years to his life, Hezekiah, however, did not use his new-found strength and health wisely. He revealed his proud heart by giving members of the Babylonian royal family a tour of all his wealth. He bragged by "telling all" to these foreign visitors, who then returned after his death, plundered the riches of his kingdom and carried the people into captivity. The prophet Isaiah had confronted Hezekiah about his action, but the king had appeared more concerned about his own image than the difficulties his descendants would face. Yet Hezekiah had a son, born to him after his healing, who became one of the most wicked kings Judah had!

What a warning to us to use our new strength and health wisely! *God did not heal you for yourself.*

God's Grace Compensates

When healing apparently does not happen, *divine grace more than compensates*. Sometimes God does not remove every physical pain or symptom, yet He will give you grace to rise above it. He will continue to fill you with His Holy Spirit, giving you energy and strength to serve Him in spite of your ailment.

You may even wonder later: "How did I do that? God didn't heal me, but still He enabled me to do that unthinkable task for Him!" We may well ask, Could it be that God gives *more grace* to those whom He has not apparently healed? Could it be that God gives *more strength* than if He had removed the ailment? You can continue to be full of God's love and grace whatever the outcome.

Kay Arthur tells the story of standing with her friends Billie and Gene at the bedside of their 41-year-old son. Mike was brain dead from encephalitis, and the time had come to remove the life-support systems. As they stood there choking back the tears, they sang and read Scripture. Billie and Gene had been confident that God was going to heal their son physically. Many others had been praying with them, but the answer God gave was not the one they wanted.

Seeing their son slipping away was especially hard for this couple, because they had no assurance that he had ever accepted Christ as his Savior. They had a promise from God but no evidence. But they kept holding on to their faith. They had trusted God for many years, and they did not stop now . . . even in their pain.

Kay Arthur concludes that this was actually a greater miracle than if God had healed Mike. Seeing the Lord restore him to physical health would have been a cause

197

for great joy. But the steadfast hope and faith of his parents in spite of the circumstances were greater testimonies to the all-sufficiency of God's grace.

We need to be like Gene and Billie—Christians whose faith does not waver, who don't serve God only when things are going well, who are lights in the darkness.[1] In the mystery of God when He has not healed us, His grace more than compensates.

God Renews Your Strength

Finally, whether the Lord heals you or not, He does renew your strength. A reporter asked Harvey on his 110th birthday, "How do you account for your longevity?"

Harvey replied, "You might call me a health nut. I never smoked. I never drank. I was always in bed and sound asleep by ten o'clock. And I've always walked three miles a day, rain or shine."

The reporter said, "But I had an uncle who followed that exact routine and died when he was 62. How come it didn't work for him?"

Harvey replied, "All I can say is that he didn't keep it up long enough."[2]

Well, praise God that whether we live long or short, our times are in His hands! *Whether the Lord heals you or not, He renews your strength.* Recall the words the Lord gave to trembling Gideon: "The Lord turned to him and said, 'Go in the strength you have and save Israel out of Midian's hand. Am I not sending you?'" (Judges 6:14).

God was saying to Gideon: "Not only am I *with* you, I, the Lord God, am *sending* you. You are a mighty warrior. Go in the strength I have given you. Go in the strength I am now giving you. Go out and do something great and mighty for Me. Surely I will be with you. Go save your people. I will be with you, enabling you. With My help, you can do it!"

This challenge may appear overwhelming. Yet this is the same message the Lord gives to all God's children.

- As God said to *Moses*: "Now go; I will help you speak and will teach you what to say" (Exodus 4:12).
- As God said to *Joshua*: "Have I not commanded you? Be strong and courageous. Do not be terrified; do not be discouraged, for the LORD your God will be with you wherever you go" (Joshua 1:9).
- As God said through *Isaiah*: "Do not fear, for I am with you; do not be dismayed, for I am your God. I will strengthen you and help you; I will uphold you with my righteous right hand. . . . For I am the LORD, your God, who takes hold of your right hand and says to you, Do not fear; I will help you" (Isaiah 41:10, 13).
- As God said through *Jeremiah*: "'For I know the plans I have for you,' declares the LORD, 'plans to prosper you and not to harm you, plans to give you hope and a future'" (Jeremiah 29:11).
- As God said through *Jesus*: "Therefore go and make disciples of all nations. . . . And surely I am with you always, to the very end of the age" (Matthew 28:19–20).

What the Lord said through the prophet Isaiah, He says to all the people of God: "You were wearied by all your ways, but you would not say, 'It is hopeless.' *You found renewal of your strength, and so you did not faint*" (Isaiah 57:10, emphasis added).

The writer of Hebrews refers to those people of faith "whose weakness was turned to strength" (Hebrews 11:34). Paul adds, "I can do everything through him who gives me strength" (Philippians 4:13).

199

From this day forward, with the new strength and health the Lord gives you, live your life fully for God and His glory. Through pain and suffering, in healing and in health, you have had an encounter with the risen and living Lord Jesus Christ. Now go and make a difference for God! Serve the Lord and others; extend Christ's Kingdom locally and globally; live life overflowing with the Holy Spirit upon you! Live your life on purpose!

Reflections

1. Why did God heal you?
2. What are you doing with your new strength and health?
3. If the Lord has not healed you, how is He supernaturally enabling you?

Prayer

God, I affirm that my health and healing are sacred gifts from You. I choose to use my strength and health for You and Your Kingdom, and not to waste them on my own selfish pleasures. Even if You have not removed pain and suffering, I affirm that You still give me an inflow of vital energy, strength and vigor. Your grace more than compensates. I am enabled to rise above it all and go on with my work. To encounter the risen Christ is to experience the grace of God and the touch of the Holy Spirit upon my life—with or without fully realizing complete healing or perfect health. To God be the glory, great things You have done! Amen.

Appendix 1

The Healing Ministry of Jesus Christ in the Gospels

Healing Stories	Matthew	Mark	Luke	John
Man with Leprosy Healed	8:1–4	1:40–45	5:12–16	
Roman Centurion's Servant with Paralysis Healed	8:5–13		7:1–10	
Peter's Mother-in-Law with a Fever Healed	8:14–15	1:29–31	4:38–39	
Two Demon-Possessed Men from Gerasenes Healed	8:28–34	5:1–20	8:26–39	
Paralytic Healed	9:1–8	2:1–12	5:17–26	
Jairus' Daughter Raised from the Dead	9:18–19, 23–26	5:21–24, 35–43	8:40–42, 49–56	
Woman Subject to Bleeding Healed	9:20–22	5:24–34	8:42–48	
Two Blind Men Receive Sight	9:27–31			

Healing Stories	Matthew	Mark	Luke	John
Demon-Possessed Mute Man Cured	9:32–34			
Man with a Shriveled Hand Restored	12:9–14	3:1–6	6:6–11	
Demon-Possessed Blind and Mute Man Cured	12:22–23		11:14	
Gentile Woman's Demon-Possessed Daughter Healed	15:21–28	7:24–30		
Demon-Possessed Epileptic Boy Healed	17:14–21	9:14–32	9:37–45	
Two Blind Beggars (including Bartimaeus) Receive Sight	20:29–34	10:46–52	18:35–43	
Demon-Possessed Man Delivered		1:21–28	4:33–37	
Deaf-Mute Man Healed		7:31–37		
Blind Man at Bethsaida Healed		8:22–26		
Widow's Son Raised from the Dead			7:11–17	
Woman Crippled and Bent Over by a Spirit Healed			13:10–17	
Man with Dropsy Healed			14:1–4	
Ten Men with Leprosy Healed			17:11–19	
High Priest's Servant's Ear Healed			22:49–51	
Royal Official's Son Dying with a Fever Healed				4:46–54
Invalid at Pool of Bethesda Healed				5:1–15
Man Born Blind Healed				9:1–41
Lazarus Raised from the Dead				11:1–44

Healing Accounts	Matthew	Mark	Luke	John
Every Sickness and Disease Healed; All Healed	4:23–24		6:17–19	
All Healed	8:16–17	1:32–34	4:40–41	
Every Sickness and Disease Healed	9:35–36			
Many Healed	11:2–6		7:18–23	
All Healed	12:15–21	3:7–12		
A Few Healed	13:58	6:5–6		
Those Needing Healing Healed	14:14		9:11	6:2
All Who Touched Jesus Healed	14:34–36	6:53–56		
Many Healed	15:29–31			
Many Healed	19:1–2			
Blind and Lame Healed	21:14			
Demons Driven Out		1:39		
Many Healed			5:15	
Women Cured and Healed			8:2	
Goal to Heal			13:32	

Appendix 2

The Healing Ministry in the Church Today

Some of you may be pastors, elders, deacons or spiritual leaders investigating the role of healing in your church. Others may be exploring the ministry of healing because you wonder if the Holy Spirit has gifted you in that area. Others may be ordinary believers who care about your sick friends and relatives. You want to see God's power heal people for His glory. Let me encourage you—the Lord uses the prayers of ordinary Christians in extraordinary ways.

In this appendix I have provided an overview of the material in this book in question-and-answer form to help you continue your exploration of the healing ministry. I have used this section as leadership development for the elders in my church in the ministry of healing.

What does the Bible say about healing?

The Bible has much to say about healing in both Old and New Testaments. The Word of God affirms that "Jesus Christ is the same yesterday and today and forever" (Hebrews 13:8). Jesus died on the cross to redeem the whole person. Isaiah *predicted* the healing ministry of the Messiah; Matthew *presented* Christ as the Healer; Peter *noted* the ongoing healing work of Christ (see Isaiah 53:4–5, 10; Matthew 8:16–17; 1 Peter 2:24). And healing continues to be *practiced* by the Church today.

Does God heal in answer to prayer today?

Yes, God heals in answer to faith expressed in prayer! Thousands of God's children have experienced the healing touch of the Great Physician. They can testify to complete deliverance from physical illness and suffering. They know that the Lord hears and answers prayer, and they give God the glory.

Is there a biblical model for the healing ministry team you describe in this book?

The following diagram illustrates the biblical basis of the healing ministry team. The *prayers of the saints* combine with the *role of healing* through trusted believers and potential *gifts of healing* through Spirit-gifted believers. Sometimes *our healing God* chooses to heal supernaturally apart from physicians, hospitals or medication. Other times the Lord uses them all.

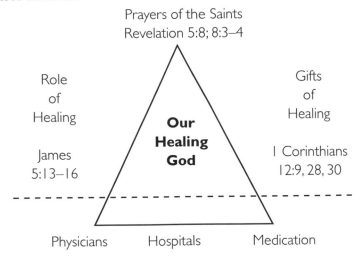

What about faith healers?

The concern about faith healers is the possibility that those seeking healing would put their faith in *them*. This is clearly erroneous because faith healers *do not* heal. That is one way many people put faith in faith. Those who are sick should seek divine healing—not just the exercise of faith, but faith in God (see Mark 11:22).

Where do I start?

It is, of course, impossible to describe every kind of situation that you may encounter as part of a healing ministry team. In some cases, you may be called to pray for an individual you do not know. The following guidelines are general procedures, especially in situations in which you do not know the sick person. As you gain confidence in the mechanics, you will learn to relax and depend on the Lord to guide you on each occasion.

1. *Gather: If you are part of a group, gather in a circle around the individual seeking prayer.* The person can be seated or standing. You can sit, stand or kneel.
2. *Identify: Make sure you know the person's name.* If you don't know the person, ask if he or she attends your church. Ask if he or she has received Christ as Savior. If the person does not know Christ, make it your first priority to lead him or her to the Savior before continuing with prayer for healing.
3. *Inquire: Find out the person's basic need.* Ask: "How may we pray for you?" Or: "Will you share with us your need? What do you want us to pray for?" Or: "What do you want Jesus to do for you?"

   The person must be precise about the *need* without going into great and perhaps private detail. Open conversation and sharing characterize this moment.
4. *Build: Stimulate the sick person's faith.* Ask: "What do you want God to do for you physically?" Read or quote the promise from James 5:15–16: "The prayer offered in faith will make the sick person well; the Lord will raise

him up. If he has sinned, he will be forgiven. Therefore confess your sins to each other and pray for each other so that you may be healed." While God responds to faith, healing does not always depend upon the sick person's faith—it may depend more upon yours. On the other hand, the person may come full of faith with a readiness for prayer. Ask then: "Do you have a word from the Lord?" His or her faith may stimulate yours.

5. *Probe: Address the sin issue, if appropriate.* Some sickness can be rooted here. Make sure there is no one against whom the sick person holds any unforgiveness or bitterness. A person cannot receive forgiveness if unforgiveness resides in his heart (see Matthew 6:14–15; 18:35).

   Ask if there is anything between the person and God that would hinder him from receiving the Lord's healing touch: "Is there anything you need to confess or make right so that you can pray without doubt?" If so, give an opportunity to confess that sin.

   On some occasions you may question an individual's *motivation*. If so, ask the person: "Why do you want to be healed?"

6. *Anoint: Explain briefly about anointing with oil.* Mention what the Bible says and describe what procedure is about to take place. Begin by saying, "Jesus taught us to lay hands on the sick and anoint them with oil to make them well." Explain to the person that the oil is a symbol of the outpoured Holy Spirit and His healing work in the sick person's body. It is a symbol; there is no power or magic in the olive oil. Anointing the sick with oil, of course, is not absolutely essential—believing prayer is!

How should I then pray for someone's healing?

1. *Touch: Lay your hands gently upon the person's head or shoulder.* If many are involved, others can lay hands on the shoulders of those in front of them. Closing your eyes to pray is not necessary—you may observe God actively at work in the person's body.

2. *Anoint: One of the pray-ers touches the person's forehead with a drop of oil.* Say: "I anoint you in the name and authority of the Lord Jesus Christ." Traditionally, and meaningfully for the sick, the sign of the cross is made upon the forehead with the anointing thumb or finger.

3. *Listen: Listen to the Holy Spirit's direction in prayer.* Healing is the work of the Holy Spirit. The Holy Spirit often gives special direction to pray as you ask Him. Spend a few moments in silence or quiet praise as you wait upon the Lord. Ask the Lord for guidance even as others are praying. "This is the confidence we have in approaching God: that if we ask anything according to his will, he hears us. And if we know that he hears us—whatever we ask—we know that we have what we asked of him" (1 John 5:14–15).

4. *Pray: Pray in faith with an attitude of praise.* The one who anointed the person with oil can lead out in prayer for divine healing. Another person can then agree in prayer. Others can also pray as the Spirit leads them. Pray in the Spirit with the Spirit's direction. Pray with authority in Jesus' name. Specific ways to pray can include:

- Affirming the finished work of Jesus Christ on the cross
- Claiming the promises of God's Word
- Speaking the word of healing
- Verbalizing an instance when Jesus healed in the gospels
- Praying a Scripture impressed on you by the Holy Spirit
- Declaring words of deliverance
- Exalting God in praise

We learn to pray as we pray. Faith is believing what God intends to do—visualize the person well! The Scripture affirms: "And the prayer offered in faith will make the sick person well; the Lord will raise him up. If he has sinned, he will be forgiven" (James 5:15). Of those who pray, perhaps only one will pray the "prayer of faith." You may sense the Holy Spirit upon you in these instances; you will know it is *God* doing the healing.

5. *Encourage: Conclude with words of faith and encouragement.* Perhaps a reassuring handshake or hug may be an appropriate conclusion.

Should particular spiritual gifts be exercised?

Those with various gifts of healing should feel the freedom to exercise them. Other gifts that are most often used when praying for the sick are faith, intercession and mercy. Once you begin to pray for someone's healing you may exercise a spiritual gift that you did not realize you had.

Is there anything special to keep in mind?

Compassion toward the person and tactful sensitivity to the person's need are always appropriate.

Depending on the individual and circumstance, you may give the person an opportunity to pray or express praise to God. Sometimes you may sing a praise song to conclude the occasion.

What if the illness returns?

If an illness returns, it may mean that the root cause that brought about the illness has not been resolved. People need to stay in fellowship with God and with His leading in their lives for their healing to be secure.

What if the person is not healed?

During prayer ministry, both the pray-ers and the one being anointed express faith and obedience. But Jesus is the healer. Never question the sincerity of the person if physical healing does not occur. On every occasion, however, some blessings will be received through a personal encounter with Jesus Christ.

God sometimes chooses to heal over a short or long period. Some people are healed instantaneously while others experience a delay. Some are healed completely while others are healed partially. Some are healed gradually or progressively. The words "They will get well" (or recover) imply that a healing process can be involved (see Mark 16:18).

Some lose their aches and pains. Others find relief through the care of doctors. Some go through surgeries. Some are not healed on earth; they must wait until heaven. The Lord may choose to overrule even our most earnest prayers for His own reasons.

Should we anoint the person again?

Absolutely! There is no reason a person should not pursue healing. Elijah prayed for rain seven times. Even Jesus prayed for a blind man twice. Paul pursued a particular need three times. In his case, he had to live with it, but that is not always the result. Especially in longstanding conditions, which encompass a variety of concerns, keep praying until the full answer comes!

How does the ministry of healing affect the Church?

In the ministry of Jesus, the blind were healed, the deaf could hear, the dumb could talk, the lame could walk, demons were cast out and even the dead were raised. Matthew described Christ's ministry of teaching, preaching and healing this way: "Jesus went throughout Galilee, teaching in their synagogues, preaching the good news of the kingdom, and healing every disease and sickness among the people" (Matthew 4:23).

The kingdom of evil showed its power, yet the power of Jesus was shown to be greater. Jesus performed signs and wonders that demonstrated His reign over areas in which Satan particularly works: sin, disease, demons, destruction and death. Jesus still demonstrates His reign in these areas.

When we pray in faith and see God dramatically answer those prayers, those answers will:

- Show people a supernatural God who works with supernatural power, who intervenes in humanity's fallen condition to speak, to help, to heal, to care

210

- Prove to the world that God is alive and at work in Christ's Church
- Motivate the unbeliever to come to Christ
- Give the believer a foretaste of the full revelation of heaven while still on earth

As Christians, we exercise Christ's delegated power to demonstrate God's wonderful love. The Lord continues to show His power to heal through prayer today!

Notes

Chapter 1   Need: *What Is Your Need?*

1. Clement of Alexandria, "The Instructor," in *The Ante-Nicene Fathers*, vol. 2, ed. Alexander Roberts and James Donaldson (Grand Rapids: Eerdmans, 1971), 210.

Chapter 2   Want: *What Do You Want Jesus to Do for You?*

1. Nigel Rees, comp., *Cassell's Humorous Quotations* (London: Cassell & Co., 2003), 346.
2. Edward K. Rowell and Bonne L. Steffen, ed., *Humor for Preaching and Teaching: From Leadership Journal and Christian Reader* (Grand Rapids: Baker, 1996), 133.

Chapter 3   Lessons: *What Is God Teaching You through This Affliction?*

1. Mrs. Charles E. Cowman, *Streams in the Desert*, vol. 2 (Grand Rapids: Zondervan, 1966), September 29.
2. Dan Matthews, "Lifestyles," *Vibrant Life*, May/June 1988, 29.

Chapter 4   Scripture: *What Do You Believe the Bible Says about Healing?*

1. Frederick W. Faber, "The All-Embracing," in *The Best Loved Religious Poems: Gleaned from Many Sources*, comp. James Gilchrist Lawson (New York: Revell, 1933), 124.
2. A. B. Simpson, *Days of Heaven on Earth: A Year Book of Devotional Readings from Scripture Texts and Living Truth* (Harrisburg, Pa.: Christian Publications, Inc., 1945), 348.

3. Mark Water, ed., *Daily Encounters: A Personal Experience of the Divine for Every Day of the Year* (Peabody, Mass.: Hendrickson, 1997), 112.

Chapter 5 Love: *Does God Really Love You?*

1. Judith Balswick and Boni Piper, *Life Ties: Cultivating Relationships That Make Life Worth Living* (Downers Grove, Ill.: InterVarsity, 1995), 165.

Chapter 6 Faith: *Will God Heal You and Heal You at This Time?*

1. This image emerges from Ezekiel's vision in Ezekiel 47:1–5.
2. Albert B. Simpson, "Yesterday, Today, Forever," in *Hymns of the Christian Life* (Harrisburg, Pa.: Christian Publications, Inc., 1978), 119.
3. Stan Guthrie, "Muslim Mission Breakthrough," *Christianity Today* 37, no. 15 (13 December 1993): 26.
4. "The Life of St. Macrina," in *Saint Gregory of Nyssa: Ascetical Works*, trans. Virginia Woods Callahan, vol. 58, *The Fathers of the Church: A New Translation*, ed. Roy Joseph Deferrari (Washington, D.C.: Catholic University of America Press, 1967), 188–90.

Chapter 7 Cause: *What Is the Underlying Cause of Your Sickness?*

1. Bob Condor, "At Ease After a Strenuous Outing Athletes Benefit from Some Time Off," *Chicago Tribune*, 23 October 1997, 10.
2. *Hope Health Letter* (Hope Health Publications), April 1996.
3. Brother Lawrence, *The Practice of the Presence of God: Being Conversations and Letters of Nicholas Herman of Lorraine* (Westwood, N.J.: Revell, 1958), 57.
4. Mention of a sickness unto death is found in 2 Kings 13:14; 20:1; and Isaiah 38:1. I did not list a sickness unto death earlier as a cause because it stands unique. I do mention it here, however, because this does influence your approach to prayer.
5. Guy Chevreau, *Catch the Fire: The Toronto Blessing—An Experience of Renewal and Revival* (Toronto: HarperCollins, 1994), 219.
6. George Vander Weit, "Hmong Believers Exorcise Evils Spirits," *The Banner*, 15 July 1996, 9–10.

Chapter 8 Barriers: *Are You Removing Barriers to Healing?*

1. "Philadelphia, New York Rank 1–2 in Survey of Hostile Communities," *Chicago Daily Herald*, 14 May 1994; quoted in *Contemporary Illustrations for Preachers, Teachers, and Writers*, ed. Craig Brian Larson (Grand Rapids: Baker, 1996), 17.

2. "Male Despair Tied to Atherosclerosis," *Chicago Tribune*, 26 August 1997.

3. Patti Davis, *Angels Don't Die: My Father's Gift of Faith* (New York: HarperCollins, 1995), 27–28.

Chapter 9 Deliberation: *Have You Thoroughly Prepared Your Inner Life?*

1. Manie Payne Ferguson, "Blessed Quietness," in *The One Year Book of Hymns*, comp. and ed. Robert K. Brown and Mark R. Norton (Wheaton, Ill.: Tyndale, 1995), May 21.

2. John G. Whittier, "Dear Lord and Father of Mankind," in *The Hymnal for Worship & Celebration* (Waco: Word Music, 1986), 427.

3. "Worship Music Crosses Water and Touches a Heart," *Send!* 14, no. 4 (July/August 1994): 2.

Chapter 10 Commitment: *Are You Ready to Give Yourself Totally to God?*

1. Candide Chalippe, trans., *The Life of St. Francis of Assisi* (New York: P.J. Kenedy & Sons, 1877), 253.

2. Margaret Murray, "Uncle Wilson's Last Words," in *His Mysterious Ways* (Carmel, N.Y.: Guideposts, 1988), 225.

3. John Wimber, *Living with Uncertainty: My Bout with Inoperable Cancer* (Anaheim, Calif.: Vineyard Ministries International, 1996), 42–44. That John Wimber himself later died of cancer is part of the mystery of God's ways.

Chapter 11 Readiness: *Which Scriptures Are You Claiming for Your Healing?*

1. Water, *Daily Encounters*, 112.

2. *George Whitefield's Journals* (London: Banner of Truth Trust, 1960), 60.

3. Larry Dossey, "Science, Prayer, and Healing," *Body Mind Spirit* 13, no. 6 (July/August 1994): 88.

4. F. W. Boreham, *A Bunch of Everlastings, Or Texts That Made History: A Volume of Sermons* (Chicago: Judson Press, 1920), 130–31. The text is Matthew 28:20, KJV.

Chapter 12 Others: *Have You Called Others to Pray?*

1. A. J. Gordon, *The Ministry of Healing: Miracles of Cure in All Ages* (Harrisburg, Pa.: Christian Publications, Inc., 1961), 65.

2. Water, *Daily Encounters*, 115.

Chapter 13 Ask: *Are You Ready to Ask God to Heal You Now?*

1. Irenaeus, "Against Heresies," in *The Ante-Nicene Fathers*, vol. 1, *The Apostolic Father with Justin Martyr and Irenaeus*, ed. Alexander Roberts and James Donaldson (Grand Rapids: Eerdmans, 1973), 409.

2. Edythe Draper, ed., *Draper's Book of Quotations for the Christian World* (Wheaton, Ill.: Tyndale, 1992), 200.

3. Francis MacNutt, "The Mystery of Healing," *Charisma & Christian Life* 14, no. 2 (September 1988): 97.

Chapter 14 Authority: *Do You Need to Exercise Authoritative Faith?*

1. Rufus M. Jones, ed., *George Fox: An Autobiography*, vol. 1 (Philadelphia: Ferris & Leach, 1906), 180.

2. Albert B. Simpson, "Healing in Jesus," in *Voices in Worship: Hymns of the Christian Life* (Camp Hill, Pa.: Christian Publications, Inc., 2003), 416.

3. Ian Hall with Joyce Wells Booze, "They Named Him Samuel," *Pentecostal Evangel* 4266 (11 February 1996): 18–19.

Chapter 15 Sensations: *Are There Further Triggers of Faith That God Gives?*

1. A. B. Simpson, ed., *A Cloud of Witnesses for Divine Healing: Second Edition* (New York: Word, Work and World Publishing Co., 1887), 139.

2. Simpson, *A Cloud of Witnesses*, 198–201.

Chapter 16 Encounter: *Is Your Authentic Faith Leading to an Encounter with the Risen Christ?*

1. St. Jerome, *Life of St. Hilarion*, trans. Marie Liguori Ewald, vol. 13, *The Fathers of the Church: A New Translation*, ed. Roy Joseph Deferrari (New York: Fathers of the Church, Inc., 1952), 254-55. We may not agree precisely with Hilarion's statement, which may imply earning grace, but we cannot deny the reality of Jesus' cure!

2. Craig Brian Larson, ed., *Illustrations for Preaching and Teaching: From Leadership Journal* (Grand Rapids: Baker, 1993), 99.

3. Benjamin Franklin, *Poor Richard's Almanack* (New York: Century Co., 1898), 83.

4. John E. Packo, *Coping with Cancer: 12 Creative Choices* (Camp Hill, Pa.: Christian Publications, Inc., 1991).

5. Robert Johnson, "Born-Again Surgeon Is at One with God but Not with Peers," *Wall Street Journal*, 6 June 1994; quoted in *Contemporary Illustrations*, 35–36.

Chapter 17 Do: *Are You Believing and Acting As Though God Has Healed You?*

1. Albert B. Simpson, "Stretch Forth Thy Hand," in *Hymns of the Christian Life*, 276.

2. George O. Wood, "Psalm 103: Deep Healing," *Pentecostal Evangel* 4355 (26 October 1997): 6.

Chapter 18 Trials: *Are You Prepared for Trials of Faith?*

1. Larson, *Illustrations for Preaching and Teaching*, 266.

2. Oscar Wilde, *Lady Windermere's Fan* (Mineola, N.Y.: Dover Publications, 1998), 5.

3. John-Julian, ed. and trans., *A Lesson of Love: The Revelations of Julian of Norwich* (New York: Walker and Company, 1988), 179.

4. Edward K. Rowell, ed., *Quotes and Idea Starters for Preaching and Teaching: From Leadership Journal* (Grand Rapids: Baker, 1996), 56.

5. Or, "I dressed him, and God healed him." *Scientific Papers: Physiology, Medicine, Surgery, Geology of The Harvard Classics*, ed. Charles W. Eliot (New York: P. F. Collier & Son, 1910), 9.

6. Amby Burfoot and Bob Wischnia, ed., "Down but Not Out," *Runner's World* 26, no. 8 (August 1991): 10.

Chapter 19 Abide: *Are You Continuing to Draw Life from the Risen Christ?*

1. Dale Carnegie, *How to Stop Worrying and Start Living* (New York: Simon and Schuster, 1948), 253–54.

2. John Stott, "Persevering Under Pressure," *Student Leadership Journal*, spring 1993, 32.

Chapter 20 Providence: *Are You Trusting Christ Even if He Has Not Healed You?*

1. *Fresh Illustrations*, 169.

2. *The Quest Study Bible: New International Version* (Grand Rapids: Zondervan, 1994), 1602.

3. Leith Anderson, *Praying to the God You Can Trust* (Minneapolis: Bethany, 1998), 97–98.

4. Oswald J. Smith, "Deeper and Deeper," in *Sing to the Lord Hymnal* (Kansas City, Mo.: Lillenas Publishing Company, 1993), 477.

5. This threefold prayer is from Stephen F. Arterburn and David A. Stoop, ed., *Spiritual Renewal Bible: New Living Translation* (Wheaton, Ill.: Tyndale, 1998), 983.

6. Elizabeth Mittelstaedt, "Afterwords: Living by God's Promises," *Today's Christian Woman* 17, no. 1 (January/February 1995): 72.

7. William Cowper, "Light Shining out of Darkness," in John Henry Johanson, *The Olney Hymns*, vol. 20, *The Papers of the Hymn Society*, ed. James Rawlings Sydnor (New York: The Hymn Society of America, 1956), 18–19.

Chapter 21   Living: *After Your Healing, Are You Living a Changed Life?*

1. A. B. Simpson, *When the Comforter Came: Thirty-one Meditations on the Holy Spirit—One for Each Day in the Month* (Harrisburg, Pa.: Christian Publications, Inc., 1911), eleventh day.

2. Lowell D. Streiker, *Nelson's Big Book of Laughter: 150 Illustrations and Thousands of Smiles from A to Z* (Nashville: Nelson, 2000), 192.

3. Leonard Sweet, "Ten Commandments for an Unhappy Life"; quoted in *Humor for Preaching and Teaching*, 176.

Chapter 22   Purpose: *Are You Using Your New Strength and Health for God?*

1. Kay Arthur, "Letter to Precept Ministries Supporters," August 1996, 1–2.

2. Streiker, *Nelson's Big Book of Laughter*, 192.

Index

abandonment, 171–84. *See also* surrendering to God
acceptance, 141–43
Acts, book of, 40
advice, seeking, 67–68, 154
affliction. *See* sickness
aging, 66, 106
American Heart Association, 79
Anderson, Leith, 175
"angel from God," embracing sickness as, 26
anger, 66, 78, 80, 81. *See also* forgiving others
anointing with oil, 42, 111–12, 114, 116–17, 134, 167, 207–8, 210
Anthony the Great, 139
anxiety, 67, 77, 81, 181
apologizing, 77, 80–81
apostles, 151–53. *See also* disciples; *individual names*; *specific topics*
Ardeleanu, Cristina, 129–30
arrogance after healing, 186–87, 196
Arthur, Kay, 197–98
asking God for healing. *See* prayer for healing; precise asking
"as-though" faith, 153–54, 156
atonement, 47
attitude problems
    as barriers to healing, 76–83
    and cause of sickness (*see* cause of sickness)
    negativity, 53

and unreadiness for healing, 34
Augustine of Hippo, 48
authoritative faith, 13, 111–12, 114, 119–20, 123–31, 161, 208
authority
    Bible as fulcrum, 38–39
    demons and our, 71
    of God, obeying, 48, 176

bad attitude. *See* attitude problems
Balswick, Judy, 52
Barnabas, 153
barriers to healing, 76–83
Bartimaeus, 102–3
Basil the Great, 63
Bath, England, waters of, 169–70
Baxter, Richard, 114–15
believers. *See* Christians
believers, gifted. *See* gift of healing, spiritual
believers, trusted. *See* trusted believers
Bethesda, invalid at pool, 69, 186, 202
Bible. *See* Scriptures
bitterness, 81, 207. *See also* forgiving others
bleeding, woman subject to, 82, 102, 201
blindness, miraculous healing of, 201–3
    Bartimaeus, 102–3
    beggar, 23–24, 28, 202
    from birth, man with, 69,

92–93, 152, 202
    daughter of soldier (healing recorded by Gregory of Nyssa), 63
    two men with, 61–62, 201
    woman from Facidia (fourth century), 139
body
    abuse to, 66, 191
    committing to God, 93–94
    divine health, 190
    Holy Spirit, as temple of, 191
    as for the Lord, 42
    mind-body relationship, 67
    sensations during prayer, 131–36
    See also whole person
body, Christians as one, 138
boll weevil, 177
born again. *See* salvation
Bosworth, F. F., 10
breathing, spiritual, 188–89
Brookes, James H., 87
Buddhism, 56
Byrd, Dr. Randolph, 104

cancer, 141–42. *See also* sickness
cardiac patients, 104
caregivers, 27
Carver, George Washington, 177
cause of sickness, 65–75, 167
    avoiding excessive focus on, 72–74
Caussade, Jean Pierre de, 175
Ceisler, Rich, 191

celiac axis compression syndrome, 174–75
charismatic gifts of healing, 11. *See also* faith healing
chemical imbalance, 71
children, 13, 112
Christ. *See* Jesus Christ
Christian and Missionary Alliance, The, 47
Christians, 211
  as one body, 138
  suffering of, 95–96, 189, 193
  unhappy, 192–93
  See also trusted believers; *specific topics*
church, local. *See* local church
church leaders. *See* spiritual leaders
cities of "hostility index," 78
Clement of Alexandria, 20
commitment to God, 91–98
common sense, 153
Communion, Holy, 187
community, 78–79, 99. *See also* local church; trusted believers
compassion, in healing ministry, 209
confession of sin, 12, 42, 69, 77–78, 82–83, 114–15, 207
conscience, overactive, 81
conversion, 143–44
counselors
  advice, seeking, 67–68, 154
  therapists (*see* doctors)
  See also spiritual leaders
Cowper, William, 183
crippled, miraculous healing of the, 201–3
  beggar at Temple, 74
  by Paul, 153
  by Peter, 132–33, 186
  See also lameness
criticism for others, 192
cross, Christ's death on, 27, 39–42, 45–46, 53, 138, 141, 204
Cummisky, Barbara, 35–36

Daily, Starr, 185
David, King, 67
Davis, Patti, 79–80
deacons. *See* spiritual leaders
deaf-mute man, 70, 202
death, 106, 142, 167, 181, 210
  of Christ on cross (*see* cross, Christ's death on)
  sickness and, 26, 68
debts, paying, 77, 80–81
DeCiantis, Beth Anne, 163
decision-making, fear- or stress-based, 77

delay in healing, 32–33, 154–55, 162–63, 165–66, 168–70, 209–10. *See also* denial of healing
demonic influence or activity, 66, 68, 69–71, 210
  physical weakness and, 79
  pressing beyond, 82
  rebuking, 77
demon-possession, miraculous healing of, 201–3
  boy, 33, 202
  epileptic boy, 49, 202
  large crowd healed, 41, 73, 203
  mute man, 70, 202
denial of healing, 27, 34–35, 166–84, 190
  and faith, 155
  and grace, 95–96, 106–7, 141–42, 197–200, 209–10
Dent, Lawrence, 149–50
depression, 40, 79
desire for healing
  refining, 23–29, 91
  tenacity and, 61–62
  and when healing doesn't happen, 27
  wishing vs. wanting, 25
desires, holy, 84, 88
desires, sinful, 77,189
desiring God, 32, 187
despair, 49, 79, 166, 191
devil, 120, 161, 210. *See also* demonic influence or activity; evil
diabetes, 162–63, 173–74
diet, 31, 66, 142, 191, 193
disciples, 33, 49, 73, 188, 199. *See also* apostles; *specific events*
discipline, divine, 66, 77
discouragement, 49, 79, 155, 160–62, 166, 191
disease. *See* sickness
disobedience, 82, 167
  sickness attributed to, 68
divine healing. *See* healing, divine
doctors, 9, 26, 115, 140, 183
  faith and common sense, 154
  God healing through, 154, 162, 210
  and healing ministry team, 205
  seeking God first, 113–14, 139
  See also individual names
Dorsey, Thomas A., 93
doubt, 26, 44, 81, 160–61, 167
  admitting, 50, 121

pressing beyond, 82, 128
and strengthening faith, 49–50, 105, 125, 167, 169, 207
as temptation, 155, 160–62, 164
Downing, Ivan, 28

eating right. *See* diet
elders. *See* spiritual leaders
Elijah, 115, 210
emotional wounds, 66, 70–71
encountering the risen Christ, 11, 13, 14, 45, 137–45, 200, 209
endurance, 141–43
epistles, 40
Eucharist, 187
evangelists, 11
Everson, Susan, 79
evil, 156, 185
  abandonment vs. acquiescing to, 176
  as mysterious, 34–35
  power of Jesus and, 210
  of sickness, resisting, 21, 25–26
  See also sin
evil spirits. *See* demonic influence or activity
excuses, 80–81
exercise, 66, 191, 193

Faber, Frederick, 42
failure to heal. *See* denial of healing
faith, 33, 39, 58–64, 105, 120, 161, 206–9
  "as-though," 153–54, 156
  authentic (*see under* faith: true)
  authoritative (*see* authoritative faith)
  climax of, 115–16
  and common sense, 154
  cultivating, 11, 13, 14, 39
  and doubt (*see* doubt)
  in faith vs. in God, 60–61, 155
  firm, 43–47
  focus, as having, 25
  gift of, 209
  growth of, 19, 33, 47–48
  in Jesus as healer, 118–22
  lack of (*see* doubt)
  misguided, 43, 46–47
  mountain-moving, 33, 125
  mustard seed, as small as, 33, 105
  "prayer of faith," 208–9
  and pressure, response to, 79

saving faith vs. healing
faith, 101
specific, 101, 105, 108–10,
119
strengthening when weak,
49–50
that "takes," 128, 130
and theological
development, 47–48
and theological scale of
divine healing, 43–47
trials of, 159–64
triggers of, 124, 131–36
true, 29, 39, 49, 60–61, 105,
143, 155, 164, 167
trusting God as, 105, 120–22
unformed, 43–47
when healing hasn't
happened (see denial of
healing)
See also faith for healing
faith for healing, 118–22,
150–51, 155–56, 167
asking for, 105
as ongoing activity, 150–51
saving faith vs., 101
what it's not, 105–6
"faith healing," 11
divine healing vs., 60–61,
206
families, 13, 112
fear, 54, 114, 155, 158, 160
decision-making based on,
77
fearing God, 55
and forgiving others, 80
help for, 188, 199
pressing beyond, 81, 82,
128
pressure, response to, 79
as temptation, 155, 160–62,
164
focus of faith, 25
forgiving others, 67, 77,
79–81, 207
Fox, George, 124–25
Francis of Assisi, 92
Franklin, Benjamin, 140

Gethsemane, Garden of,
175–76, 178–79
"getting right with God,"
80–81
Gideon, 198
gift of healing, spiritual, 112,
113, 205, 209
goal of seeking healing, 13,
135, 137–45
God, 35, 45
desiring, 32
glorifying, 28, 29, 119–20,
121, 157

and questioning human
suffering, 34–35
Kingdom of, 35, 167, 195,
196, 200, 210
listening to, 27, 33, 47, 103,
107, 164–70, 210
power of, 61, 139, 169
sovereignty of, 35, 44–46
surrendering to (see
surrendering to God)
as wanting to heal, 45
will of, 33, 107–8, 125, 128,
175–77, 180
Word of, written (see
Scriptures)
See also Jesus Christ;
specific topics
God's love, 32, 52–57, 60, 86,
105, 107, 167, 211
personalizing, 20, 53–56
good health. See health
good people, suffering of, 34–
35, 95–96, 189, 193. See
also denial of healing
Gordon, A. J., 10
gospels, the, 40
healing ministry of Christ
in, 56, 201–3
See also Scriptures
grace of God, 35, 54, 67,
169–70, 187, 200
for endurance, 16, 107, 141,
144, 167, 172–73, 197–98
giver of, becoming, 195
for healing, 141–43, 196
trusted believers as
channels, 115
gratitude, 90
attitude, and health, 67
for healing, 186
"Great Physician," Christ as,
11, 20, 39, 67, 74, 116,
163, 205
Gregory of Nyssa, 62–63
grudges. See forgiving others
guided liturgical practices, 11
guilt, 66, 78

Habakkuk, 107
habits, 66, 67, 74, 77, 78,
82, 142
good, to cultivate, 190
mental (see thoughts)
Hall, Ian, 129–30
Hallesby, Ole, 121
hand, shriveled, miraculous
healing of, 151, 202
hatred, 80, 81
healing, divine, 15, 34, 105,
140–41, 157, 162–63,
187, 195
after, 185–200

as in atonement, 47
barriers to, 76–83
basis for, 48, 138
before, 11, 13, 16–98
delay in, 32–33, 154–55,
162–63, 165–70
denial of (see denial of
healing)
desire for (see desire for
healing)
faith healing vs., 60–61, 206
gift of, spiritual, 112, 113,
205, 209
as glorifying God, 28, 29,
119–20, 121, 157
goal of, 13, 137–45
and God's will, 107
and health, 106
Holy Spirit and, 94, 138–40,
208
immediate, 134, 135, 162
invisible, 106
life after, 185–200
loss of, 186–87
motivation for, 28
mystery of, 14, 36, 88, 95–
96, 104–5, 114, 121, 172,
198
of non-believers, 47, 95–96
obedience, principle of, 153
partial, 162–63
prayer for (see prayer for
healing)
preparation for, 11, 13, 16–
98
psychological, 40
purpose of, 194–200
readiness for, 101–9
at resurrection, 95–96, 141,
145, 174
sin after, 196–97
as still happening today, 14,
205
testimonies of others, 38
theological scale of, 42–47
and touch, 56–57, 118, 207–8
unreadiness for, 34
when it doesn't happen (see
denial of healing)
See also Jesus Christ as
healer; specific topics
healing faith, 118–22, 150–51,
155–56, 167
asking for, 105
as ongoing activity, 150–51
saving faith vs., 101
what it's not, 105–6
See also faith
healing ministry, 12–13
in the Church today, 204–11
of Jesus Christ, 41, 103, 132,
201–3, 210

New Testament, 151–54
procedures, guidelines for, 206–9
team, 205
health
attitude and, 78–80
church attendance and, 79
divine, 190
healing and, 106
living in, after healing, 187
Healy, Kathy, 174–75
heart-attack patients, 104
Henderson, Joe, 65
Hezekiah, King, 196
Hilarion, 139
Hilary of Poitiers, 71
His Mysterious Ways (Murray), 95–96
Holy Spirit, 41, 48–51, 53, 59–60
body as temple of, 191
breath of, 188–89
disciplinary work of, 77
faith and, 105
healing and, 94, 138–40, 208
listening to, 208
prayer and, 114, 124, 127, 128, 208
temptation and, 161
See also specific topics
honesty, and seeking healing, 21
hopelessness. See despair
hormonal problems, 71
hostility, 78. See also anger
human suffering, 34–35
humility, 34, 186

Ignatius Loyola, 169
illness. See sickness
immediate healing, 134, 135, 162. See also miracles of Jesus
immune system, 78–79
impure thoughts and motives, 77
"indifference," 169
inferiority, feeling of, 53
"infirmities," 39. See also sickness
injury, 66. See also sickness
inner life, preparing, 84–90
instantaneous healing, 134, 135, 162. See also miracles of Jesus
intercession, 209
invalid at pool of Bethesda, 69, 186, 202
invisible healing, 106
Irenaeus, 118
Isaiah, 199

James, 12, 42, 115
Jeremiah, 199
Jerome, 139
Jesus Christ, 27, 39–41, 59–60, 138, 199
Garden of Gethsemane, 175–76, 178–79
life in, 186–88, 190
risen, encountering, 11, 13, 14, 45, 137–45, 200, 209
See also cross, Christ's death on
Jesus Christ as healer, 13–14, 34, 39, 41, 73–74, 82, 103, 118–22, 201–3
faith in, 118–22
large crowd healed of diseases, 73, 203
love for the sick, 56–57
ministry of, 210
today, 45
See also "Great Physician"; miracles of Jesus
Job, 26, 35, 68, 106
John (the apostle), 74, 195–96.
See also specific topics
Johnson, Clara, 116
Johnson, Clinton, 113
Johnson, Robert, 143–44
John the Baptist, 99
Joshua, 199
joy
after healing, 186
attitude of, and health, 67
Julian of Norwich, 161–62

Kingdom of God, 35, 167, 195, 196, 200, 210

lameness, miraculous healing of, 201–3
George Fox reporting, 124–25
See also crippled
Lawrence, Brother, 67
laying on of hands. See touch
Lazarus, 167
leaders, spiritual. See spiritual leaders
leprosy, miraculous healing of, 56, 201–3
man with, 56, 132, 201
ten men with, 21–22, 152, 202
lessons learned through sickness, 30–37, 189
life after healing, 185–200
Lincoln, Abraham, 120
liturgical practices, guided, 11
Livingstone, David, 108
Living with Uncertainty (Wimber), 97–98

Lloyd-Jones, D. Martyn, 162
local church, 12, 42, 113
attendance, link to health, 79
healing ministry in, 204–11
Lord's Prayer, 128
Lord's Supper, 187
loss of healing, 186–87
love of God for you. See God's love
loving relationships, 78
Luther, Martin, 127–28
Lydia (magazine), 180–83

MacNutt, Francis, 10, 121
Macrina (sister of Basil the Great and Gregory of Nyssa), 62–63
Mangano, Frank and Mary, 135
Mary, 178
Mcarthy, Rev. John, 150
McClure, John, 97
McWhorter, Michael, 144
meaninglessness, 78
medical treatments
faith and common sense, 154
See also doctors
mental anguish, 40
mental habits. See thoughts
mental illness, 66, 70–71
mercy
of God, 22, 24, 42, 45, 54
as spiritual gift, 209
Michelangelo, 192
Mikelson, Vera, 123
Miller, Duane, 156–57
ministry, healing. See healing ministry
ministry leaders. See spiritual leaders
miracles, 48, 97–98, 125
miracles of Jesus, 201–3
specific, identifying with, 103
See also specific miracles, e.g. paralyzed man, miraculous healing of
Mittelstaedt, Elizabeth, 180–83
Montillana, Oscar, 88–89
Morscheck, Rev. Duane, 26
Moses, 41, 199
motivation
for healing, 25, 28
impure, abandoning, 77
mountain-moving faith, 33, 125
Murray, Andrew, 10
Murray, Margaret, 95–96
Muslims, 61

Index

mustard seed, 33, 105
Myconius, Friedrich, 127–28
Myer, Richard, 124–25
mystery of healing, 14, 36, 88, 95–96, 104–5, 114, 121, 172, 198

need
God as knowing, 31
identifying and acknowledging, 19–22, 206
physical and spiritual, 19
negativity, 53
overcoming, 77, 88
See also attitude problems
neurological problems, 71
New Testament
ministry of healing, 151–54
See also Scriptures
Nicolson, Harold, 24
nonbelievers, 211
health and healing of, 47, 95–96

obedience
to God, 77, 81
in healing, principle of, 153
ten men with leprosy, 22
occult activity, 77
old age, 66, 106
Old Testament. See Scriptures
olive oil, anointing with. See anointing with oil
Overton, Dr. Marvin, 143–44

Packo, John, 141–42
pain, 31, 34
living with, 180–84
See also sickness
Palmer, Rev. Sack, 150
paralyzed man, miraculous healing of, 81–82, 151, 201
Paré, Ambroise, 163
parents, 13, 112
partial healing, 162–63, 209–10
pastors. See spiritual leaders
patience, 34
waiting on the Lord, 191
Paton, John G., 87–88
Paul, 143, 168, 195, 210
healing crippled man, 153
"thorn in the flesh" of, 172–74
See also specific topics
peace, inner, 87
Penney, J. C., 166
Pentecost, 188
persistence, 61–62, 163–64
Peter, 74, 178
healing crippled man, 132–33, 186

physical body. See body
physical healing. See healing
physicians. See doctors
pleasure of God, living for, 191–93
pool of Bethesda, invalid at, 69, 186, 202
Pool of Siloam, 92, 152–53
praise, 85, 88–89
attitude of, and health, 67
prayer and, 208, 209
prayer, 107, 208–9, 210–11
authoritative, 123–30
Holy Spirit and, 114, 124, 127, 128, 208
of Jesus at Gethsemane, 178–79
in Jesus' name, 127–28, 133
listening for God's answer, 27, 33, 47, 107, 164–70, 173, 210
progressive steps in, 179–80
of a righteous man, 12, 42, 115
true, 126–27
prayer for healing, 11–14, 113
after, 11, 14, 147–200
before, 11, 13, 16–98
cause of sickness and, 68
during, 13–14, 99–145
guidelines for, 207–9
by others, 11–13, 99, 110–18, 124–25, 137, 190, 205
precise asking (see precise asking)
sensations during, 131–36
and touch (see touch)
three phases of, 13–14
visualization, 208–9
for yourself, 110, 114
See also healing, divine
prayer ministry, 12–13
"prayer of faith," 208–9
prayers of the saints, 110, 205
precise asking, 22, 118–22, 206
preparation for healing, 11, 13, 16–98
pressure
excuses and, 80–81
handling, 77
self-destructive responses to, 79
pride, 28, 81, 173
priorities, reordering, 81
promise of God, 167
providence, divine, 171–84
psychological healing, 40
psychological problems. See emotional wounds; mental illness
purpose of healing, 194–200

Quest Study Bible, The, 172
quietness, 84–90

readiness for healing, 101–9
Reagan, Ronald, 79–80
realization, 179–80
reason for healing, 194–200
refining desires, 23–29, 91
relationships
loving, 78
strained, 77, 79
See also forgiving others
release, 179–80
repentance, 68, 86
resentment, 66, 77–78, 81.
See also forgiving others
resolve, 179–80
rest, adequate, 191
restitution, 77, 80–81
resurrection of the body, 95–96, 141, 145, 169, 174
resurrection life, 139–41, 187
resurrection of Jesus, 138, 142, 188
return of sickness, 189, 209
Revelation, book of, 40
risen Christ, encountering, 11, 13, 14, 45, 137–45, 200, 209
Runner's World, 163

sacrifice, living
Christ as (see cross, Christ's death on)
giving yourself to God as, 93–94
saints, prayers of, 110, 205
salvation, 14, 48, 120, 133, 169
healing ministry and, 206
saving faith vs. healing faith, 101
sanctification, 48
Sanford, Agnes, 10
Satan, 161, 210. See also evil
satanic attacks. See demonic influence or activity
saved. See salvation
scale of divine healing, 42–47
Scriptures, 31, 38–50, 204–5
after healing, 187
faith and, 39, 58–59, 101–9
self-destructive responses to pressure, 79
self-doubt, 53
selfishness, 81
self-pity, 24, 79
sensations during prayer, 131–36
sensitivity, in healing ministry, 209

shriveled hand, miraculous
    healing of, 151, 202
Shua Cha, Pastor, 72
sickness, 20–21, 156, 210
    and attention from others,
        24
    cause of, 65–75, 167
    demonic attack and, 69–71
    embracing as "angel from
        God," 26
    enjoyment of, 24
    forgetting, 32
    lessons learned through,
        30–37
    pain, living with, 180–84
    resisting as evil, 21, 25–26
    return of, 189, 209
    and self-pity, 24
    sin and, 68–69, 77–78, 207
    symptoms, 66, 70, 82, 155,
        158, 160, 194
    and virtue, 34
Siloam, Pool of, 92, 152–53
Simpson, Albert B., 10, 47,
    59–60, 128–29, 134, 153,
    188–89
sin, 66, 210
    after healing, 186–87, 196–
        97
    as barrier to healing, 76–78,
        82
    confessing, 12, 42, 69, 77–
        78, 82–83, 114–15, 207
    and "infirmities," 39
    repentance for, 68, 77
    and sickness, 68–69, 77–78,
        207
sleep (adequate rest), 191
Smith, Oswald, 176
Society of Jesus, 169
sorrows, 40
Sor Thao, 71–72
soul. See inner life; whole
    person
specific faith, 101, 105,
    108–10, 119. See also faith
    for healing
speed of healing, 162–63. See
    also delay in healing
spirit
    spiritual and physical
        nature, 20, 67
    See also whole person
Spirit, Holy. See Holy Spirit
spiritual breathing, 188–89
spiritual gift of healing. See
    gift of healing, spiritual
spiritual leaders, 13, 111,
    113

spiritual life, 188–89
    deepening, 33
    See also faith
stasis, 85
Stott, John, 167–68
strength, God as giving, 94,
    98, 138–43, 145, 155, 169–
    70, 180–81, 186–200
    to equal your days, 167
stress, 77
    self-destructive responses
        to, 79
suffering. See human
    suffering; sickness
suicide, 181
supportive believers. See
    trusted believers
surrendering to God, 33, 94,
    98, 171–84, 178, 190, 193.
    See also abandonment
Sweet, Leonard, 191–92
symptoms, 66, 70, 82, 160,
    164
    ignoring, 155, 158

tact, in healing ministry, 209
Temple, crippled beggar at, 74
temptation, 160–62, 181
    doubts and fears as, 155
tenacity, 61–62, 163–64
"Ten Commandments for an
    Unhappy Life," 191–92
theological development,
    47–48
theological scale of divine
    healing, 42–47
therapists. See doctors
"thorn in the flesh," 172–74
thoughts
    attitude problems (see
        attitude problems)
    habits and patterns, 67, 77,
        88
time concerns, 162–63. See
    also delay in healing
Today's Christian Woman,
    180–83
touch, 56–57, 118, 207–208.
    See also miracles of Jesus
trials of faith, 159–64
triggers of faith, 124, 131–36
true faith, 39, 49, 60, 143, 155,
    164, 167
    and specific faith, asking
        for, 105
    what it's not, 61
    See also faith

trusted believers, prayer of,
    11–13, 99, 110–18, 124,
    137, 190, 205
    encouragement for, 125
    procedure for, 114
    trusting God, 94, 105, 111,
        115, 120–21, 126, 191
    delayed healing and, 165,
        170–84
    during and after healing,
        155, 158

unbelief. See doubt
unbelievers. See nonbelievers
"unbelieving generation," 49
unhappiness. See attitude
    problems; "Ten
    Commandments for an
    Unhappy Life"
unreadiness for healing, 34
unworthiness, feelings of, 53

vacation, 192
visible healing, 106
visualization, prayer and,
    208–9

Waldensian movement,
    medieval, 112
Wallace, Rick, 21
Wall Street Journal, 143–44
wanting to be healed. See
    desire for healing
Wesley, John, 101
Whitefield, George, 103
Whittier, John Greenleaf, 87
wholeness, 14, 20, 45, 60, 128,
    153, 169, 189
whole person, 20, 40, 67, 85,
    131, 190–93, 196
    committing to God, 93–94
Wiens, Jordon, 140
Wilde, Oscar, 160
Williams, Dr. Redford, 78
will of God, 33, 107–8, 125,
    128, 175–77, 180
Wimber, John, 97–98
woman subject to bleeding,
    82, 102, 201
Woodberry, Dudley, 61
Word of God, written. See
    Scriptures
word of knowledge, 126
worry, 67, 77, 81, 181. See
    also fear
wrong living, 34
    barriers to healing, 76–83
    blamed for sickness, 68
    See also sin

The Rev. David J. Smith has served as a Christian and Missionary Alliance pastor for more than twenty years in New York State, Ontario, Canada and now Minnesota.

He met his wife, Donna, while doing undergraduate studies at Canadian Bible College in Saskatchewan. Their children, Élysa and Clayton, are college students.

He completed an M.Div. at Alliance Theological Seminary in Nyack, New York, and a Th.M. in Christian Spirituality through the University of Toronto. He is also an adjunct professor at Crown College in St. Bonifacius, Minnesota.

David plays a mean game of racquetball and likes to read. His heart and mind are on fire for God and for people.

If you would like to share your story of how God healed you, please write to:

Rev. David Smith
2105 Roselawn Ave. W
Roseville, MN 55113
pastordave@rosehillcma.org
651-631-0173